C. T. PAULSON

MAN
— OF —
WAR

M. J. PAULSON

M. J. Paulson Publishing
mjpaulson@abnorth.com

Copyright © 2024 by Marguerite Paulson
First Edition—August, 2024

Cover and Interior Design by Donna Antkowiak
Editing by Andrew Wilmot

ISBN
978-1-9994927-1-7 (Paperback)

1. BIOGRAPHY
2. RELIGION/Missionary
3. HISTORY/China

Distributed to the trade by the Ingram Book Company
Printed in the USA

Table of Contents

Photographs

Map

For we wrestle not against flesh and blood,
but against principalities, against powers,
against the rulers of the darkness of this world. . . .
(Ephesians 6:12)

For there is a war for the souls of men ". . . be vigilant;
because your adversary the devil, as a roaring lion,
walketh about, seeking whom he may devour."
(I Peter 5:8)

I

Conversion

To every man there openeth
A way and ways and a way.
And the high soul climbs the high way
And the low soul gropes the low
And in between on the misty flats
The rest drift to and fro
But to every man there openeth
A high way and a low
And every man decideth the way his soul will go.

JOHN OXENHAM[1]

It was a Sunday evening. A young man walked quietly down the street, his shoulders slightly stooped. The man heard the sound of gospel singing and stopped and slowly turned his head in the direction of the music. Intrigued, he stepped inside the church to listen. After the singing had ended, he remained for the sermon and, at the close of the service, stepped forward in answer to an alter call.

The young man's name was Clifford Theodore Paulson. He was twenty-three years old.

---

[1] Quoted by Isobel Kuhn (1997), p. 1.

II

Roots

A noble life is not a blaze
Of sudden glory won.
But just an adding up of days
In which good work is done.[2]

Clifford Paulson was born on a farm near Bawlf, Alberta, on May 5, 1907. He was the third of five children born to Bernard and Gertrude Paulson. As was common amongst pioneer women on the Prairies, Gertrude delivered all her children at home.

Bernard's father, Gulbrand,[3] was born in 1844 in the Gran district of Hadeland in Norway. Situated some thirty-five miles north of Oslo, Hadeland at the time was a broad expanse of dense forests interspersed by rolling hills and lush green valleys. The soil was rich and fertile, which made it some of the best farmland in Norway.

Gulbrand's family were tenant farmers called "husmand." In exchange for obligatory labour on a farm, husmand were given a small plot to farm for themselves.

Coat of arms of the Gran community in Hadeland to which Clifford's family belonged. The image on the shield depicts the twin towers of the Gran sister churches built during the late 12th Century.

---

2 Kuhn (1997), p. 244.

3 The English translation would be Gilbert. In the Norwegian patronymic naming system, each person had three names: a given first name, a second name derived from the father's first name followed by son or sen for a son and datter for a daughter, and a last name denoting the farm where they were born or worked. As an example, Gulbrand's father was Paul Gulbrandsen Almseiet, with Alm being the farm name and seiet the word indicating he was a labourer on the farm. In turn, Gulbrand's name at birth became Gulbrand Paulson Almseiet. In the mid 1800s the farm or third name was dropped as well as the generational change of the second name.

In the early 1800s, Hadeland experienced a rapid increase in population, and then, in the 1860s, suffered a severe drought. Unable to make a good living and adequately provide for their families, Norwegian emigrants left in large numbers for the United States. Some of these early immigrants became the fur traders and mountain men of the North American Rockies. They were rugged men, used to the mountains, deep snow, and harsh conditions, and they could travel long distances with great speed on their snowshoes.

On May 4, 1877, Gulbrand and his fiancée, Johanna, left Norway aboard the ship *Hero* and travelled to Liverpool, where they boarded a second ship bound for the United States. At first they settled in Wisconsin, where Gulbrand worked as a farm labourer until he could buy his own land. Then in 1900, they moved to South Dakota. Finally, in 1904, they followed their son, Bernard, to Canada where Bernard and his wife had gone to obtain some of the homestead land available in Alberta.

Clifford's mother, Gertrude, or Gertie as she was affectionately called, was of English extraction. She and Bernard met at a dance and were married shortly thereafter on December 27, 1887. Later, they would entertain together at barn dances and community functions where Bernard would play the fiddle and Gertrude the piano while they called out the dances. They settled near Bawlf, where Bernard farmed for a while before buying and operating a small hardware store. Later he sold the business and bought another hardware store, this time in Cadogan. Other business ventures followed, including purchasing the mineral rights on a piece of land near Wainwright; more land near Edmonton, in what is now the Bonnie Doon district; and even some land in Texas, which turned out to be swampland full of alligators. Then came the Great Depression and he lost most everything he owned when he extended credit at his store only for such debts to go unpaid.

Gertrude acted as a midwife in the area, travelling by horseback to assist the local doctor in delivering babies, mending broken bones, performing minor operations, and sewing flesh wounds. When the doctor was unavailable, Gertrude travelled alone across the Prairies to perform the necessary medical procedures, with her black medical bag perched on her horse and her sandy-coloured hair braided and wound around the top of her head.

In a heritage book titled *Prairie Echoes*,[4] Clifford recounted his parents' early life on the Prairies.

I REMEMBER – by Clifford T. Paulson

Someone has said that a country is not likely to be any richer than its early inhabitants make it. I therefore wish to pay tribute to the contribution which my father, whose parents came from Norway, and my mother, whose ancestors hailed from England, made to the Province of Alberta, and particularly the community of Cadogan where they resided for 27 years (1912–1939).

In 1904 my father, Bernard Paulson (commonly known as "Ben"), then 29, decided to emigrate with mother, 25, and their 2 children, Hazel 6 and Vernon 2, from South Dakota to Alberta where cheaper land and the prospects for farming seemed much brighter. He headed North alone in early June by freight train, a journey of 3 weeks, taking with him 4 horses, a wagon, 2 oxen, a couple of cows, some rough lumber and household things. The trip terminated at Wetaskiwin (Indian name for the neighboring Peace Hills where a peace treaty had been signed in 1867 after a fierce and exhausting battle between the Cree and Blackfoot). He then proceeded by team and wagon to Bawlf, a smaller community 50 miles East, where he filed for homestead land, began to cut brush and fell trees, and prepare the soil for the eventual seeding of grain. A small 20 x 20 sod-log shack was erected with the help of kind bachelor neighbors. My mother, Gertrude, with Hazel and Vernon, arrived about a month later. The loss of their trunk of clothing for 3 months greatly complicated life, it being necessary for the children to be put to bed in the daytime occasionally while their clothes were washed and dried. The meagre resources of the family were augmented by trapping muskrats and selling the hides for cash to purchase much needed food, implements and supplies. Within a year or so they were able to erect a more comfortable two-storey house. Three boys were eventually born, myself (Clifford), Gordon and Stewart, the farm having been sold and the family moved into the town of Bawlf, where father had operated the livery stable for a short time and then purchased the Tooky Hardware and Undertaking, thus realizing his lifetime ambition.

---

4 Hillcrest Heritage Society, pp. 118–120.

In 1912 a new opportunity presented itself at Cadogan (named after George Henry, 5th Earl of Cadogan, British statesman), a community to which many settlers were being attracted, hence the business at Bawlf was sold and the move made to Cadogan, then a village of 30 or so inhabitants which was struggling to establish itself. Father was joined in partnership by his brother, Ted, and the sign reading "Paulson Brothers Hardware" proudly nailed above the front entrance of a larger building erected on main street, (Ted later went into the garage business). My 3 brothers, Vernon, Gordon and Stewart, all gave valuable help in this hardware store for a number of years. Hazel, our sister, married John Engel and became a hard-working housewife and mother of 2 children, Stan and Glee, on the family farm 1 mile west of town. . . .

Some of the early developments of the village, which I as a very small boy fondly remember, were the CPR water-tank with its spike and large ball on top: the reddish railway box-car, with the name "CADOGAN" painted below the little window at each end in large white letters, which served as a shelter until a proper station was erected: . . . a combination pool hall—barber shop operated by friendly Waltus Lotzer: a small general store and lumber yard . . . the grocery and dry-goods store of James Murdock and Alex Spence: a second grocery store, directly across main street from father's hardware. . . . There was also a CPR section-house: . . . a one-room school for Grades I to VIII, moved from its first site on the Emil Riedel farm 1 mile East, with Miss Lila Graham of Provost as my first teacher, under whose tutorship and encouragement I was able at the age of 5 to capture first prize in the penmanship competition at the Provost Fair, a trophy which my parents proudly displayed in our home for many years: a livery stable: . . . Mrs. Hall's boarding house, well-known to travellers for its homey atmosphere and tasty meals (I recall how, as a small boy, I used to stand sometimes at her window and wish that I might be invited inside just once to taste her good food): the little tailor shop of Mr. MacEwan: . . . the blacksmith shop of Martin Neste, an accomplished violinist who played in the local dance orchestra with mother (piano) and John Engel (drums): a hotel . . . the Chinese Café of Mah Hong (Henry) and Mah Don (Harry): two churches—United and Roman Catholic: and still later a branch of the Canadian Bank of Commerce, an imposing brick building with a staff of 5, which was eventually closed and transformed into the Red Lion Hotel.

Those early days were not without their times of humor. The owner of the lumber yard, attired only in a suit of red underwear was feeding his pigs early one morning when suddenly an angry sow charged him, ran between his legs and carried him on her back around the yard for several minutes. And then also the time one of the Chinese attempted to remove the scent bag from a dead skunk and the knife slipped, cutting the bag, and sending him scurrying and making it necessary to destroy a lot of chocolates, candy and foodstuffs.

There were times of fun and excitement, too, such as snaring gophers during the summer on the big hill directly behind the village, and tobogganing there during the winter months: or the coming of Chautauqua in the fall, when the big, brown tent was pitched on the edge of town and the great outside world came to our door in the person of famous lecturers, entertainers and musicians: or the baseball games during the quiet summer and fall evenings: and always the annual Cairns picnic on May 4th—a delightful family affair!

But there were also times of heartache and sorrow. Father, who also was the local undertaker, was occasionally called to get the body of some lonely and discouraged pioneer who had taken his life (we as children talked in hushed voices and avoided walking past the store for a day or so while the body was kept in the back room awaiting burial). There were several fatal accidents during those years, too—Alex Engel killed by a train on the railway crossing East of town: a farm boy suffocated while digging for coyote pups in a sandy hillside; and the little Findlay girl, who backed into an open well and drowned while playing in the farmyard (hers was the very first funeral I attended, and I still can see in my mind's eye her little gravestone surmounted by a small white lamb on her grave in the Lutheran cemetery North of town). I have vivid memories of the anxious days when the flu epidemic struck down everyone except my father and mother and a certain Mr. King, and how my mother, a practical nurse, worked tirelessly night and day (alone, or with Dr. York of Provost) to comfort and relieve the sick, the only loss of life being the wife of Joseph Emil, clerk in the Brownlee and Lockyer store.

Perhaps the greatest tragedy to strike the community was the drought and depression of 1929 to 1939, "Ten Lost Years" as one farmer called them, "when the country blew right from underneath our feet, taking our precious soil North, South, East and West, never to come back!"

The weather turned upside down and the economy flopped. Thousands of wheat-growing acres burned out, banks and mortgage companies foreclosed hapless farmers and ranchers, resulting in families turning their backs on their hard-won land and walking away, leaving large debts unpaid on the books of local merchants (my father told me once that he had lost about $75,000). A great, rich land went without rain for several years, the burning sun sucked off all moisture and dried up the crops, winds blew mercilessly vibrating even the houses, and the topsoil was lifted for miles into the sky, obscuring the sun and turning day into a veritable night. Everything in the gardens just grew a little and then died of thirst. The vulnerable economy of the prairies collapsed. Wheat, which sold during the earlier flush years at $1.70 to $2.00 a bushel, plummeted to 38¢. Eggs went at 5–10¢ a dozen. While my wife and I were doing missionary work in Northern Alberta under the Canadian Sunday School Mission, a farmer with whom we were staying showed us a cheque for 65¢ which he had received for a 5-gallon can of cream which he had shipped to Edmonton by express. Although many people found new strengths and became unusually resourceful, their lives were forever scarred by the Dirty Thirties.

For me the curtain on this dismal scene was mercifully drawn by my departure for China in 1934 with my wife, Florence Bradley (who once taught school, as I also did, at Blackhill), and our ten-month old son, Philip, where we served as missionaries with the China Inland Mission. God later gave us 3 more boys (Keith, Blake and Duane) and 3 girls (Elaine, Lucille and Marguerite). While in China I received the sad news of the death of my brother, Stewart, and when we returned to Canada on furlough in 1944 my father and mother had moved from Cadogan to Edmonton, where they were trying to pick up the pieces of their lives and make a feeble but brave new start. Both now have passed on and we only have the memories. Despite their broken dreams, they were not embittered by the struggles, hardships and disappointments of the 27 years spent in Cadogan, but rather were grateful to God for having had the privilege of making a small but honest contribution to the early life of one of Alberta's great but unsung communities.

III

Disposition

The Lord will perfect that which concerneth me: thy mercy, O
Lord, endureth for ever: forsake not the works of thine own hands.
(PSALMS 138:8)

Clifford was a special joy to his mother. Although not the best looking of her four sons, he was a quiet, gentle man, studious and intelligent, and an avid reader on a number of subjects. Each day when coming home from school, he would sling several large books over his shoulder to read at night, which rendered his left shoulder shorter than his right. His favourite subjects were Ancient History and English Literature, particularly the works of Charles Dickens. The themes of conflict between moral righteousness and the degradation of man appealed to him. There was *Oliver Twist*, which depicted the principle of good surviving through manifold adversity and triumphing in the end; and *David Copperfield*, where the weak and helpless were hopelessly abused by the strong and powerful.

Other tales of Dickens' spoke to the moral redemption of the intransigent soul. There was the alcoholic Sydney Carton in *A Tale of Two Cities*, who sacrificed his life by the guillotine to save Charles Darnay, the husband of the woman he loved. By Carton's death in service to save another, his own life finally gained meaning and value. Another recalcitrant soul was Ebenezer Scrooge, the sour old miser from *A Christmas Carol*, who realized his inanity and became a benefactor of the poor. In all likelihood, it appears that Dickens' portrayal of man's need for redemption struck deep into the core of Cliff's being. He may even have seen himself as one of Dickens' unfortunate characters.

Clifford read the dictionary religiously, learning at least one new word a day and incorporating it in various sentences until he had committed the word to memory. Thus in his later years, when recalling words that began with "s," the family's cat was named Squiffy.

Clifford was a very talented young man. He was athletic and excelled in a number of sports, and he was also an active spectator. He was artistic and used black Indian ink with a pen or brush to create masterful sketches and pieces of calligraphy. One of his sketches hangs in an art gallery in Hong Kong. He was musical, too, and a good dancer, having as a child attended many a barn dance at which his parents performed. He excelled at pool and used his knowledge of geometry to become a more than competitive player. As a young man he had no problem making money by clearing the pool table when his turn came. He liked horse racing and regularly watched the Triple Crown. He even attended the local race track, going in to the stables to view the horses and converse with the trainers and jockeys. His favourite was William Shoemaker, a famous American jockey, who he went to meet on a layover flight. While in church, Clifford would draw pictures of Clydesdale horses to keep his small children occupied and very, very quiet.

Clifford was a knowledgeable man with varied interests ranging from the arts to politics. He followed fashion trends from Paris and New York and regularly perused *Vogue* magazine. He kept abreast of political issues and world events and frequently wrote letters to the editors of various newspapers, and to world leaders, too, to comment on current events. At one time he carried on a lively correspondence with Gordon Sinclair, the avowed atheist from *Front Page Challenge*. On another occasion he wrote a letter to a Tel Aviv newspaper in which he defended Israel's position on a world issue. His letter was published and caught the attention of then–Israeli Prime Minister Menachem Begin who invited him to visit the parliament in Israel.

Clifford was principled and was not embarrassed to stand for what was right. Once while watching a baseball game, he caught a fly ball and would not return it despite the jeers of the crowd. At the end of the game, he quietly went to the umpire and turned in the ball. When asked why he did not return it earlier, he said in effect we do not follow the crowd, but we still do what is right.

All in all, Clifford was a talented young man: a man of abilities and capabilities who would have excelled at anything he pursued. There were no limits to his possibilities. In Psalms 49, verse 18, it says, ". . . men will praise thee, when thou doest well to thyself," but then it goes on to say in verse 20, "Man that is in honour, and understandeth not, is like the beasts that perish."

IV

Bible Training

Plaudits of men we lightly appraise,
Set we a nobler aim—
Ever to bring through the toil of the days
Glory to God's great Name.
Many the voices that ring in our ears,
Many the cries of need;
God give us grace in the coming years
His voice alone to heed.

Plaudits of men we lightly appraise,
Set we a nobler aim—
Ever to bring through the toil of the days
Glory to God's great Name.[5]

After finishing high school at Provost, Clifford enrolled at the Teachers Training College in Camrose, defraying some of the costs of his education with monies wagered and won by playing billiards. It was there that he first met his future wife, Florence.

In a brief autobiographical account titled "Roots," Clifford wrote:

(After graduation), I taught in 2 schools but decided to get other work as the winters were cold and the pay low, so I went to Edmonton where I worked as cashier at General Trust, then on to Calgary where the climate was warmer and got a job as a de-coder with California Fruit Growers Exchange (all business was done by secret code between California and the Calgary office). At that time Florence's sister, Frances, was married

---

[5] The words and music of this hymn were composed by S. Houghton, one of the missionary teachers at Chefoo School, recorded in Gordon Martin's book, *Chefoo School 1881–1995*, p. 11.

and living in Calgary so Florence visited her occasionally. It was in Calgary then that we met again and began to go together seriously. We attended the young peoples meetings and Sunday services at the Prophetic Bible Institute Church where Dr. Imrie was pastor.

We decided to be married at the parsonage on Saturday February 7th of that year, 1931, then went off to Banff by train for a weekend honeymoon. In Calgary we had rented a small upstairs suite in a private home at the corner of 6th Avenue and 8th Street S.W. (close to the downtown core). While living there we came in contact with various missionaries who visited Calgary and felt called to offer ourselves for missionary services abroad. Accordingly I gave up my job and we vacated the little suite and left for Three Hills for Bible training to prepare for missionary work.

Upon marriage, Florence negotiated that if and when they had children, and if he was at home, Clifford would get up with them, make their breakfasts, and get them off to school. She also negotiated that she would have her own bank account and monies. All of this was rather unusual in the 1930s, but Florence had been raised by a very independent, widowed British mother who was a strong believer in women's rights. Clifford kept his promise to her.

In the fall of 1931, Clifford and Florence commenced their studies at Prairie Bible Institute (PBI) in Three Hills, Alberta. Three Hills was a small village of about five hundred people situated on the desolate prairie of central Alberta. The College was started in 1922 by a group of Christian farmers headed by Fergus Kirk. Fergus felt burdened by the need for a local Bible school for young people. The winters there were long with little work available, which meant there was ample time for Bible study. The college was to be interdenominational with no affiliation to any one church or denomination. An old abandoned farm house served as the first school for eight students, each of whom was boarded by a local farmer.

Later, a building site was purchased on the edge of town and a regular school was erected. All materials were donated and voluntary labour was provided by a small group of farmers. Even during the Depression, they supported the college as well as various missions, using monies from selling their car, if they had one, or foregoing buying one and walking to town or driving a horse and buggy instead. They dispensed with further conveniences that would have made their lives much easier.

To offset tuition and other costs of attending Bible school, the students helped with maintenance and operational work. Clifford served on the dish crew in the kitchen, which likely accounted for his later disinclination to do dishes—though by then, he had a number of children who were regularly assigned that chore.

Studies at the college included the Bible, doctrine, apologetics, ancient history, evangelism, children's ministries, English, and music. In addition, there were weekend Bible and mission conferences. Missionaries from the Sudan Interior Mission presented their work in Africa, the China Inland Mission (CIM) presented their work in China, and the Canadian Sunday School Mission presented their Bible camps for children.

Clifford was not raised in a Christian home and had not been exposed to the Bible and its teachings. After his conversion, he immersed himself in studying the scriptures and was able to shed light on them for others. At PBI, one of his classmates, a young man by the name of Walter McNaughton,[6] had applied to serve as a missionary under the Sudan Interior Mission. As part of his candidacy application, Walter:

> . . . had to write a paper giving his own personal doctrinal statement. In it he wrote that he believed hell was eternal, but he wasn't too sure that people would be always there. He told his classmate, Cliff Paulson about it. Cliff said, "Walter, remember that in Daniel it says, 'Many that sleep in the dust of the earth shall wake, some to everlasting life and others to shame and everlasting contempt.' That same word for everlasting is used there."[7]

Because of their age and educational qualifications, Clifford and Florence were able to complete the usual three-year program at PBI in two and graduated in spring 1933. Their first child, Philip Timothy, was born five months later. It was during their time at PBI that Clifford felt the call of God to serve as a missionary in China.

---

[6] Walter McNaughton went on to found the Peace River Bible Institute at Sexsmith in northern Alberta.

[7] Thiessen, p. 64.

V

Calling

No one has the right to personalize the promises and privileges of the Gospel without personalizing the obligations and responsibilities.[8]

"Go, therefore and make disciples of all nations" . . . The Lord commands us saying I have sent you to be a light . . . that you may bring salvation to the uttermost parts of the earth. As Dr. Speer observed so many years ago, how can we claim for ourselves Christ's "Come unto me" and claim exemption from his "Go"?[9]

Clifford's call[10] to China as a missionary was distinct and clear. There was no doubt about it—he wanted to serve God and felt led to serve him in China. It was not an impetuous decision, but one fuelled by gratitude to a God who had provided him salvation for what he realized was a sin-based life. In his writings, Clifford laid out two reasons for missionary work, the first being an internal reason: a "sense of deep gratitude and love makes us missionary-minded." He stated, "All that I am I owe to Him," and quoted II Corinthians 5:14–15:

> For the love of Christ constraineth us; because we thus judge, that if one died for all, then were all dead:
>
> And that he died for all, that they which live should not henceforth live unto themselves, but unto him which died for them, and rose again.

---

8 Quote by Dr. Vincent Brushwuler, recorded by Clifford in a file marked "Missionary Sayings."

9 Lucia Cozzens, a missionary martyr in Cameroon in 1949. Newell, p. 115.

10 J. Bentley Taylor, in an article titled *The Call of God*, defined a calling as "the continual sense that a certain course is God's will and that (the person) must do that and not anything else."

Clifford noted that there was no inherent difference between himself and the pagan of Africa or China and asked, "Why was I not a heathen worshiping idols and demons?" His response was, "Only due to the grace of God."

Gratitude is one of the reasons why educated and talented young men and women like Clifford and Florence gave up everything and went to foreign countries to preach the gospel. They had received salvation and God's grace, which had such an impact on their lives that they wanted to share it with others. No matter the cost to them personally, they did not consider their efforts spent seeking lost souls a "waste." Their desire was to give all in return for all that they had been given.

The second reason, Clifford proffered, was external: the lost souls of the world. In his testimony printed in *China's Millions*, November 1934, he wrote:

> I might say that the condition of the millions in the unreached regions, who are dying without the Saviour, and my consequent responsibility to those who "are carried away unto death, and those that are ready to be slain" (Proverbs 24: 11, R.V.) rested heavily upon my heart ever since I was saved.
>
> Hence I am pouring out my life to Him in love upon the alter of service trusting that He will use it in winning back the precious souls for whom Christ died. (p. 173)

The lost souls of China had also been the burden of Hudson Taylor, leading him to found the CIM to which Clifford had been accepted. In the early 1850s, Hudson wrote to his mother:

> Think, Mother, of twelve million—a number so great that it is impossible to realize it—yes, twelve million souls in China, every year, passing without God and without hope into eternity. . . . Oh, let us look with compassion on this multitude! God has been merciful to us; let us be like Him . . . [11]

---

[11] Taylor (1932), p. 31.

The most important reason for missionary service, however, is the direct and clear command of Jesus to "Go ye into all the world, and preach the gospel to every creature."[12] As Fanny Crosby[13] wrote:

Rescue the perishing,
Care for the dying,
Snatch them in pity
From sin and the grave;
Weep o'er the erring one,
Lift up the fallen,
Tell them of Jesus,
The mighty to save.

Hudson Taylor noted that,

The privilege of carrying the saving message has . . . been entrusted exclusively to us. What then can we say if our master returns today and finds that after nineteen centuries, more than half the world is utterly unevangelized? The gospel to every creature—a plain command. Millions who have never heard it—a simple fact. What are you going to say? . . . What explanation can we give, other than to hang our head in shame.

Although salvation is secured by faith alone, judgement is still rendered for man's works. To accept God's grace and not reach out a hand to the unsaved is a sin. In the Old Testament, God gave Ezekiel this command:

When I say unto the wicked, O wicked man, thou shalt surely die; if thou dost not speak to warn the wicked from his way, that wicked man shall die in his iniquity; but his blood will I require at thine hand.[14]

The command to "Go" requires obedience and entails a responsibility. Hudson Taylor said, "Are you willing to obey in everything, every time,

---

12 Mark 16:15.
13 Fanny Crosby, a blind hymnist, wrote the words for "Rescue the Perishing" in 1869. Fanny had been asked to speak to a group of blue-collar workers in Cincinnati. Near the end of her address, she had the overwhelming feeling that a young man in the audience needed to be rescued that night, or not at all. She mentioned this to the crowd and pleaded for the young man, whoever he was, to come and see her at the close of the meeting. He came and ultimately was saved. Later that night, Fanny, in pondering over the deep need to "rescue the perishing," wrote out the words for the hymn. At age 60, Fanny moved to lower Manhattan, close to the Bowery, and continued her rescue work. (Morgan, pp. 174–75).
14 Ezekiel 33:8.

everywhere?" Obedience to God's command requires action. A person may have compassion, but without action, compassion is a useless emotion.

> . . . if my Saviour calls, shall I not obey? If He has left his throne in glory to come and bleed and die for us, shall we not leave all, and follow Him?[15]

Isobel Kuhn, a CIM missionary to the Lisu in the western mountains of China, noted that many other tribes were asking for missionaries to come to their area. One tribe waited over ten years. Isobel commented on the delay:

> Do you think that when they called for gospel messengers, God did not respond? It could not be. He gave His most precious son that all might know and receive eternal life. I think that man did not respond. It costs something to leave loved ones and the comforts of civilization. I believe that each generation God has "called" enough men and women to evangelize all the yet unreached tribes of the earth. Why do I believe that? Because everywhere I go, I constantly meet with men and women who say to me, "When I was young I wanted to be a missionary, but I got married instead." Or, "My parents dissuaded me," or some such thing. No, it is not God who does not call. It is man who will not respond! . . .
>
> "My flock lacks a shepherd and so has been plundered and has become food for all the wild animals and . . . my shepherds did not search for my flock but cared for themselves rather than for my flock" (Ezek. 34:8). . . .
>
> Oh, will you not help point out to the terrified little Nestlings,[16] that behind them is the Cleft of the Rock, so close, so sheltering, but so unseen unless you and I go to them?[17]

Isobel continued her admonition in her book *Second-Mile People*.

> Those Christians who love themselves better than Him, better than thousands of those who are perishing for want of what they have more than they can use (the love and saving power of Christ)—how dare such face eternity with those thousands of despairing eyes fixed on them, and those voices ringing in their ears. . . . Surely those voices will rise up

---

[15] Taylor (1952a), p. 140.
[16] Isobel Kuhn is referring to the Lisu tribes nestled on the mountains surrounding the Salween Gorge where they lived.
[17] Kuhn (1997), pp. 300–01.

again at the last day, and accuse such selfishness? . . . those who might bring them the love (of Christ) . . . are sitting at home, putting in time over puny nothings, regardless of the bitter cry that comes over the sea to them.[18]

Numerous other missionaries and Christian writers have expressed similar sentiments.[19]

In recalling a painful memory, Hudson Taylor spoke of a Chinese convert, Nyi, who asked him,

"How long have you had the Glad Tidings in England?"

The missionary was ashamed to tell him, so he tried to pass it over by saying that it was several hundred years.

Nyi was thunder-struck and cried out in surprise:

"What! Several hundred years! Is it possible that you have known about Jesus so long and only now have come to tell us? Why, sir, my father sought the truth for more than twenty years, and died without finding it."

Then with a sigh in his voice that spoke the pain of his heart he added:

"Oh, why did you not come sooner?"

Why? Can any one answer Nyi's question?[20]

As seen, God's command to "Go" requires obedience and action; it entails responsibility, and with responsibility comes accountability. In James 4 verse 17, it says, "Therefore to him that knoweth to do good and doeth it not, to him it is sin."

The mission field is all-encompassing and everyone is called to be a missionary whether abroad or at home. And if active service is not possible, there is always prayer, personal witness and financial support.

For what is the value of a soul? The cost is the blood of the Lamb. How then can believers be so careless about people's souls, given such great cost? In illustration, Hudson Taylor recounted an incident from 1856, when travelling by boat from Shanghai to Ningpo.

---

[18] Kuhn (1982), pp. 152–54.
[19] Appendix B.
[20] Kerr, p. 201.

Among his fellow-passengers, one Chinese, who had spent some years in England and went by the name of Peter, was much upon his heart, for, though not unacquainted with the Gospel, he knew nothing of its saving power. . . . Nearing the city of Sung-kiang, they were preparing to go ashore together . . . when Mr. Taylor in his cabin was startled by a sudden splash and cry that told of a man overboard. Springing at once on deck he looked round and missed Peter.

"Yes," exclaimed the boatmen unconcernedly, "it was over there he went down!"

To drop the sail and jump into the water was the work of a moment; but the tide was running out, and the low, shrubless shore afforded little landmark. Searching everywhere in an agony of suspense, Mr. Taylor caught sight of some fishermen with a drag-net—just the thing needed.

"Come," he cried as hope revived, "come and drag over this spot. A man is drowning!"

"Veh bin," was the amazing reply: "It is not convenient."

"Don't talk of convenience! Quickly come, or it will be too late."

"We are busy fishing."

"Never mind your fishing! Come—only come *at once*! I will pay you well."

"How much will you give us?"

"Five dollars! only don't stand talking. Save life without delay!"

"Too little!" they shouted across the water. "We will not come for less than thirty dollars."

"But I have not so much with me! I will give you all I've got."

"And how much may that be?"

"Oh, I don't know. About fourteen dollars."

Upon this they came, and the first time they passed the net through the water brought up the missing man. But all Mr. Taylor's efforts to restore respiration were in vain. It was only too plain that life had fled, sacrificed to the callous indifference of those who might easily have saved it.

Hudson Taylor went on to say:

Is the body, then, of so much more value than the soul? We condemn those heathen fishermen. We say they were guilty of the man's death— because they could easily have saved him, and did not do it. But what of the millions whom we leave to perish, and that eternally? What of the plain command "Go ye into all the world and preach the Gospel to every creature," and the searching question inspired by God Himself, "If thou forbear to deliver them that are drawn unto death and those that are ready to be slain; if thou sayest, Behold, we knew it not; doth not He that pondereth the heart consider it? and He that keepeth thy soul doth not He know it? And shall He not render to every man according to his works."[21] [22]

---

[21] Taylor (1952b), pp. 4–6.
[22] Appendix C.

VI

Mentor: Hudson Taylor

Great is Thy faithfulness!
Great is Thy faithfulness!
Morning by morning new mercies I see;
All I have needed Thy hand hath provideth—
Great is Thy faithfulness, Lord unto me![23]

The mission field to which Clifford felt called was China, and the mission he chose to serve under was the CIM. It had been founded in 1865 by Hudson Taylor when he deposited ten pounds into a London bank account of that name. Clifford agreed with the tenets set out by Hudson, feeling they were well-based in scripture and offered a sound model for missionary service and Christian life.

Hudson Taylor was born in 1832 in Barnsley, Yorkshire, in England. At seventeen he was converted and, shortly thereafter, felt God's call to China. Hudson was a frail young man and small of stature. Realizing that missionary work entailed significant hardship and endurance, he set out to prepare himself for the task. As in any work, Christian or otherwise, preparation is always the first step. Hudson began by exercising regularly and walking wherever he needed to go. Any conditions comparable to those he would experience in China were incorporated into his life. He simplified his diet, eating only the basest and coarsest of foods—brown bread and oatmeal, to which he occasionally added a few seasonal vegetables. Because of his meagre diet, he was able to save most of his income, which he faithfully gave to missions, sometimes as much as two-thirds of it.

Hudson did not want to be tied down to worldly possessions or trapped by the comforts of life. He divested himself of his feather bed and superfluous

---

23 A hymn written by T. O. Chisholm in *Melodies of Praise*, p. 216.

furnishings, including books and clothes. He also moved from his comfortable lodgings to a single twelve-by-twelve room in a poor, dismal part of town.

To further prepare himself, he read everything available on China and began a study of the written language. His method of study was ingenious. After obtaining a Chinese copy of the Gospel of Luke and, by comparing the Chinese characters with the English text, he was able to ascertain the meaning of the characters. Within a few weeks he had mastered over 500 Chinese symbols. He studied medicine—anatomy, physiology and surgery—believing that medical training would be an asset in his work. He also studied Latin, Greek and Hebrew in order to develop a thorough understanding of the Bible. And he prayed regularly for China. Then, with whatever time he had left, he did Christian work: distributing tracts, teaching Sunday School, and visiting the poor.

Strengthening his spiritual life and learning to rely on God alone for all his needs was a priority for him.

> To me it was a very grave matter . . . to contemplate going out to China, far from all human aid, there to depend upon the living God alone for protection, supplies, and help of every kind. I felt that one's spiritual muscles required strengthening for such an undertaking.[24]

Hudson began by leaving the matter of his finances completely in God's hands. He did not tell anyone of his need, only God in prayer. He reasoned that if only God knew, then any fulfillment of his needs could only be from God. And God always provided, not necessarily abundantly, but certainly sufficiently![25]

Hudson's faith was further honed while travelling to China. Off the coast of England, the ship encountered a catastrophic storm with violent winds and turbulent seas that spilled over the sides of the deck. All was felt to be lost. Although Hudson prayed, he was reluctant to put on a life jacket, believing that it showed a lack of faith in God's ability to protect. Later, when reflecting on his decision to give his life jacket away, he realized that when God provides the means and a person does not avail himself of those means, it degrades the matter to a test of God's power. In writing about this experience, he said,

---

[24] Taylor (1952a), p. 131.
[25] Appendix D.

The use of means ought not to lessen our faith in God, and our faith in God ought not to hinder our using whatever means He has given us . . . .

When in medical or surgical charge of any case, I have never thought of neglecting to ask God's guidance in the use of appropriate means. . . . But to me it would appear as presumptuous and wrong to neglect the use of these measures which He Himself has put within our reach, as to neglect to take daily food and suppose that life and health might be maintained by prayer alone.[26]

Further clarity on this matter is detailed in a whimsical story of a man caught in a flood. The man climbs to the roof of his house for safety and prays to God for rescue. Several people come by in a boat and ask him to get in, but he refuses. Then a life jacket floats by, but he refuses to reach for it, even though it is well within his grasp. Finally a helicopter comes by and hovers overhead, and a ladder is let down for him to ascend, but again he refuses. This continues until the flood waters rise above the roof of the man's house and he drowns. Upon arriving at heaven's gates, the man asks God, "Why didn't you rescue me?" to which God replies, "I sent you a boat and a life jacket and a helicopter. Why didn't you use them?"

As Hudson was learning to rely more and more on God to meet his needs, he continued to pray for more faith. Eventually he came to realize that it was not a matter of him needing more faith but of counting on God being faithful. "If we believe not, yet he abideth faithful: he cannot deny himself."[27] Like Hudson, Clifford relied on God to supply all of his needs, not only financial but other needs as well including protection for himself and his family.

---

[26] Taylor (1952a), p. 191.
[27] II Timothy 2:13.

VII

Mission Affiliation: China Inland Mission

Preliminary advertisement for missionary service in China:

> . . . . *If you want hard work and little appreciation; if you value*
> *God's approval more than you fear man's disapprobation; if you*
> *are prepared to take joyfully the spoiling of your goods, and seal*
> *your testimony, if need be, with your blood; if you can love the poor*
> *Chinese . . . you may count on a harvest of souls now and a crown*
> *of glory hereafter "that fadeth not away," and on the Master's*
> *"Well done."*[28]

In founding the CIM, Hudson Taylor's focus was on evangelizing the unreached interior of China. The mission was to be interdenominational, drawing from various faiths that had a set of core beliefs. These beliefs included the divine inspiration and authority of the Bible, the Trinity, man's nature of sin, atonement through the substitutionary death of Jesus, the resurrection, justification by faith, eternal life for the saved, and damnation for the unsaved.

In selecting candidates for the mission, Hudson focused more on their spiritual lives than their educational or intellectual qualifications, as was wont of other missions. Although Clifford was educated he agreed that a spirit-directed life was most important.

"While thankful for any educational advantages that candidates may have enjoyed," (Hudson) wrote, "we attach far greater importance to spiritual qualifications. We desire men who believe that there is a God

---

28 Taylor (1952b), p. 269.

and that He is both intelligent and faithful, and who therefore trust Him; who believe that He is the Rewarder of those who diligently seek Him, and are therefore *men of prayer*. We desire men who believe the Bible to be the Word of God, and who, accepting the declaration 'All power is given unto me,' are prepared to carry out to the best of their ability the command, 'Go . . . teach all nations,' relying on Him who possesses 'all power' and has promised to be with His messengers 'always,' rather than on foreign gun-boats though they possess some power; men who are prepared, therefore, to go to the remotest parts of the interior of China, expecting to find His arm a sufficient strength and stay. We desire men who believe in eternity and live for it; who believe in its momentous issues whether to the saved or to the lost, and therefore cannot but seek to pluck the ignorant and the guilty as brands from the burning."[29]

Hudson Taylor was concerned that a large number of potential missionaries were not being accepted because they did not meet the formal educational standards of other missions, and he wanted to draw from this pool. Single women were also being excluded as it was felt that, without the protection of a husband and with their frail natures, they should not be subjected to the rigors of pioneer life in China. Hudson accepted both as missionary candidates— the less educated and the single woman—and made no attempt to minimize the difficulties they would face.

China is not to be won for Christ by self-seeking, ease-loving men and women. Those not prepared for labour, self-denial, and many discouragements will be poor helpers in the work. In short, the men and women we need are those who will put Jesus, China, souls first and foremost in everything and at all times: life itself must be secondary— nay, even those more precious than life. Of such men, of such women, do not fear to send us too many. Their price is far above rubies.[30]

One such mission hopeful was a one-legged man who Clifford wrote about.

The story is told about the late J. Hudson Taylor who was one time visiting in the United States. One day when Mr. Taylor was walking down one of the streets of the city, he was accosted by a young man. The young man stopped Mr. Taylor on the street and said, "Pardon me but

---

[29] Taylor (1952b), p. 268.
[30] Taylor (1952b), p. 156.

aren't you Mr. Taylor the missionary from China?" And Mr. Taylor said, "That's right, my name is Hudson Taylor and I am from China. What is it you want?" And then the young man looked up into Hudson Taylor's face and said, "Mr. Taylor, I want to go to China to preach the Gospel to the many there who have never heard about Christ." But just then Mr. Taylor happened to glance down toward the ground and he saw that the young man had only one leg, and so he quietly said, "Young man, you have only one leg and it is not likely that you shall be able to go to China with only one leg. How is it that you, a man with only one leg should want to go to China as a missionary?"

The young man with tears in his eyes looked up into Hudson Taylor's face and said, "Why you know there are so many two-legged fellows who aren't willing to go as missionaries that I thought I should offer to go even though I have but one leg." Ah yes, listen young people, that one legged man got to China. Hudson Taylor saw that that young man had something which many didn't have, and so he was accepted as a missionary for China. He went to the field and did a great work for God at a place called Wenchow in Chekiang. I have been to that city and have seen the strong native church which he established there, and I have stayed in the very house which was built by that same one-legged missionary. God used him mightily among the Chinese and today there is a flourishing Christian church there at Wenchow, one of the best in the whole province of Chekiang. I have been told that his favourite verse was this, "The lame shall take the prey"—"The lame shall take the prey." What prey are you going to take for the Lord? You may be lame. You may not have great talents, but God is looking for obedient and humble channels. What are you doing with the gifts and talents He has given you? You have two legs, a strong body, a sound mind, health and education. Why not yield to Him today? It is not a matter of how long we serve God. It is not a matter of how popular your service is in the sight of our fellow-man, But How faithful!

Hudson did not want to appropriate prospective missionaries from other missions. He was simply looking for additional missionaries. No one was ever to be asked to join—prayer was the only method of solicitation. "If the Lord of the harvest wanted them in that particular field, He would put it in their hearts to offer." Nor was the mission to duplicate the work of any other respected mission already established in the field; it was only to work in the unevangelized parts of the country. It was to be an itinerant mission. Once an area was evangelized it was to be left for other missions to develop, and the CIM missionaries would move on to a new area.

Prayer was the keystone of the mission, and God answered Hudson's prayers. Hudson prayed that the interior of China would be opened to the gospel. At that time in China, foreigners were not allowed inland, but then God opened the door. At various times Hudson prayed for specific numbers of missionaries, one time one thousand new missionaries, and the exact numbers came. He prayed for funds; they were supplied, all in answer to prayer and faith that "God's work done in God's way will never lack God's supplies,"[31] and "God, alone is sufficient for God's own work."[32]

Hudson's calling was to preach Christ to the Chinese people—nothing more, nothing less. He asked his missionaries to adopt Chinese dress and, where not contradictory to the Bible, their customs. He likened it to Christ arriving from heaven to become man and "in all things . . . to be made like unto his brethren."[33]

> In language, in appearance, in everything not sinful He made Himself one with those He sought to benefit. . . .
>
> I am not alone in the opinion that the foreign dress and carriage of missionaries (to a certain extent affected by some of their pupils and converts), the foreign appearance of chapels, and indeed the foreign air imparted to everything connected with their work has seriously hindered the rapid dissemination of the Truth among the Chinese. And why should such a foreign aspect be given to Christianity? The Word of God does not require it; nor, I conceive, could sound reason justify it. It is not the denationalisation but the Christianisation of this people that we seek. We wish to see Chinese Christians raised up—men and women truly Christian, but withal truly Chinese in every right sense of the word. We wish to see churches of such believers presided over by pastors and officers of their own countrymen, worshipping God in the land of their fathers, in their own tongue, and in edifices of a thoroughly native style of architecture. . . . If we really wish to see the Chinese such as we have described, let us as far as possible set before them a true example. Let us in everything not sinful become Chinese, that we

[31] Taylor (1932), p. 120.
[32] Guiness (1894 I), p. 241.
[33] Hebrews 2:17.

may by all means "save some." Let us adopt their dress, acquire their language, seek to conform to their habits and approximate to their diet as far as health and constitution will allow. Let us live in their houses, making no unnecessary alteration in external form, and only so far modifying their internal arrangements as health and efficiency for work absolutely require.[34]

Hudson did not want to divert any monies initially designated for other missions, only additional monies. The CIM was to make no appeal for financial assistance; there was to be no collection of monies at meetings or services. The mission was to be sustained solely in answer to prayer:

> . . . to wait upon the Lord for the supply of every need, and to trust Him to incline the hearts of his own people to send in, unasked, just as much or as little as He would have them send.[35]

The mission was never to go into debt or obtain anything on credit. If there was no money for something, even food, it was not purchased.

> If the Word taught me anything, it taught me to have no connection with debt. I could not think that God was poor, that He was short of resources, or unwilling to supply any want of whatever work was really His. It seemed to me that if there were lack of funds to carry on work, then to that degree, in that special development, or at that time, it could not be the work of God.
>
> To me it seemed the teaching of God's word was unmistakenly clear; "Owe no man anything." To borrow money, to my mind, a contradiction of scripture—a confession that God had withheld some good things, and a determination to get for ourselves what he had not given.[36]

Whatever donations came in were to be used to meet the mission's needs. What was left over was to be divided equally among the missionaries, men and women alike.[37] No regular salaries were promised.

Clifford was deeply impacted by Hudson's life of faith and prayer and its exemplification in the principles of the CIM. Both he and Florence followed

---

[34] Taylor (1952b), pp. 90–91.
[35] Guiness (1894 I), p. 240.
[36] Taylor (1952a), p. 430.
[37] At that time, the equal distribution of monies between male and female missionaries was novel and quite controversial, as any work done by a missionary wife was typically subsumed under the salary of her husband.

these principles throughout their lives. They had no debt: no mortgage for a house, no loan for a car, no borrowing money even for food. One time while back in Canada, when the only food in the house was potatoes, Florence thoughtfully made them into French fries to make them more appealing and sprinkled them with vinegar (except the vinegar had been diluted and was more water than vinegar). But their children remembered it as one of their best meals ever.

Hudson never took any monies from the mission for himself. His own expenses were kept separate and paid for by a small trust fund of his wife's and the occasional donation designated for his personal use.

This humble young man sacrificed all to serve the Lord in China—a good income as a medical doctor in London, the comforts of a home, his health, and the loss of his first wife and three children, all buried in his adopted land. He relied on the promise of God's faithfulness. And if he gained any fame or respect at all, it was because he put God first in all things and at all times. Oh, that we could be as faithful!

VIII

Travel to China

No man, having put his hand to the plough, and
looking back, is fit for the kingdom of God.

(LUKE 9:62)

While waiting for word of their acceptance as missionaries with the CIM, Clifford did pastoral work at Wimborne, a small village near Three Hills, Alberta. He was also asked to start a bible college in northern Alberta, at Sexsmith, but had refused stating, "No, I want to try the door of China first."[38]

Acceptance to the mission came through in the summer of 1934. The young family moved to Vancouver to attend candidacy school. Upon completing their coursework, they made their final preparations to leave for China.

The young couple was stepping out in faith. It had to be faith, for why would a young man take his wife and child to a foreign country half-a-world away, an alien country where there were no conveniences or comforts or even family, and where he had no guaranteed income or understanding of the language? To remain in Canada would be easier. Both were well educated and had good family ties, not to mention all the comforts of life at their fingertips. But they stepped out in dedication and faith that God would meet their needs.

On September 15, 1934, Clifford, Florence, and ten-month-old Philip set sail from Los Angeles, travelling on a Norwegian freight ship, the *M.S. Corneville*, across the Pacific for China. The trip would take four weeks.

For most of the trip the weather was warm and the passengers only needed to wear light clothing on deck. But three weeks into the voyage, the wind started to blow against the current, forcing great waves to spill over the sides of the ship. All port holes were closed, and Clifford and his young family

---

[38] Thiessen, p. 72.

were confined below deck. Then, early in the morning, there was a great crash as a huge wave broke over the ship. The freighter stopped and began drifting out into the Pacific. At 5:00 a.m. there was another horrific crash. The boat shuddered and plunged sideways; more water started to fill the vessel. In the Paulsons' cabin, a small fire broke out and smoke filled the air. The electric light fuse blew, leaving them in complete darkness. Philip started to cry. While Florence tended to him, Clifford crawled out of his water-soaked bed to see what he needed to do. Despite the precarious situation in which they found themselves, the couple experienced incredible peace and calm, for hadn't God said, "When thou passest through the waters, I will be with thee; and through the rivers, they shall not overflow thee . . . For I am the Lord thy God . . . thy Saviour." (Isaiah 43:2–3)

On October 15, 1934, after a month at sea, the family finally docked at Shanghai. At last they were in China, a country of 450 million people and four million square miles of land. Sailing into Shanghai, they noticed that the waters were filled with fishing boats and sampans—small flat-bottomed skiffs on which people lived and traversed the waterways of China. All cooking, washing, and sleeping were done onboard, with only a tiny little cover over part of the skiff for protection. Washing was hung on lines strung across the front of the sampan or hung on long bamboo poles sticking out from the end. Typically the boats were propelled by long poles but could also be propelled by sails, towed behind another larger vessel, or hauled by ropes from shore.

Shanghai at that time was a major seaport and commercial centre situated in Kiangsu Province on the east coast of China. Three million souls lived there. As ships pulled into the harbour, tall elegant buildings seemed to rise out of the water.

The city was actually comprised of two separate and distinct communities. There was commercial Shanghai, which contained the business sector with its banks, hotels, and shops; the manufacturing sector with its warehouses, shipyards, and mills; and a residential sector with European-styled houses. The international settlement was located there, housing foreign diplomats and businessmen. It was sectioned by nationality with the CIM headquarters situated in the British quarters.

Commercial Shanghai was very European in its appearance, with some of the buildings having been transported from Paris and London and reassembled in Shanghai. Covering 5,362 acres it had all the conveniences of a modern city—broad, paved, well-lit streets, an efficient police and sanitary system, hospitals and schools. A fine esplanade, or Bund, skirted the riverbank with the city proper laid out alongside. Opposite the Bund was an attractive park with a sign that read "No dogs or Chinamen allowed." It was a city controlled by European investment and management, and home to a substantial number of foreigners under the civil, criminal, and political jurisdiction of their consuls.

Then there was the old Chinese part of Shanghai with its narrow, winding, open-sewaged streets teeming with people, rickshaws,[39] and the occasional sedan chair.[40] The merchant shops opened right onto the street and were closed off at night by vertical shutters. Along the streets Chinese workers made wadded quilts and clothing, cooked and sold food, and changed money. There were also the ever-present beggars. In the nearby river, Chinese men in small boats, called junks,[41] fished and plied their various trades. Everything overwhelmed the senses: the noise; the jostling, pushing, and shoving of the crowds; and the foul smell in the air. Most disturbing was this stench—a constant smell of urine mixed with sweat, grime, rotten vegetables, fish, and the entrails of various animals.

Upon disembarking from the *Corneville*, the family transferred to a small boat that transported them and their luggage to the customs and immigration offices. From there they went to the CIM headquarters. The mission compound was surrounded by a wall and contained green lawns and flowers and a large six-storied building of light-coloured stone and stucco. Balconies with iron rails edged each suite of rooms. Arched windows decorated the top floor, which housed a small but well-equipped hospital for mission staff and missionaries. This was the hospital where Florence's next two children would be born.

The family spent five full days in Shanghai, attending meetings with mission leaders, doing a bit of sightseeing, and preparing for their next step

---

39 A two-wheeled carriage with a long bamboo pole on each side pulled by a man called a coolie. The rickshaw could seat one or two people.

40 A chair attached on each side with a long bamboo pole. The poles were carried on the shoulders of two coolies, one at the front and one at the back. Sometimes a curtained canopy would be placed over the chair to ensure privacy for the occupant or shade from the sun. If distance or speed were required, a third coolie would accompany the others as a relief carrier.

41 A small shallow-hulled boat propelled by a sail.

of missionary life—language school. Necessary supplies were bought: head coverings, which are necessary in China, to screen out the scorching sun; wadded gowns for Florence; and mosquito nets for their beds. Clothes for Philip were obtained from an English organization called Helping Hands. Now they were ready to travel inland to Hwaining, the city where the CIM men's language school was located.

IX

Sacrifice: But not counted loss

Banish our worldliness, help us to ever live with eternity's values in view.[42]

Although Clifford and Florence had arrived in China, they had yet to start any actual missionary service. Mentally they knew that life there would not be easy, but any sacrifice was miniscule compared to God's command to "Go." Already they had experienced their first sacrifice when they left their loved ones back in Canada. But had not Jesus said that anyone who wanted to be His follower must love Him more than their own father, mother, wife, children, brothers or sisters, "yea, and his own life also"?[43] Then there was Jesus' promise for obedience:

> Verily I say unto you, There is no man that hath left house, or parents, or brethren, or wife, or children, for the kingdom of God's sake,
> Who shall not receive manifold more in this present time, and in the world to come life everlasting. (Luke 18:29–30)

In leaving Canada, Florence left a widowed mother and siblings, not knowing if she would ever see them again. Clifford had also left family behind, though they were displeased with him going into mission work—as the scholar of the family, his parents had "higher" hopes for him. "Why go to China?" "Why waste your time there?" Once on the mission field, the only family contact would be by mail, which typically arrived months later or not at all. Shortly after they left, Clifford and Florence had their wedding presents appropriated

---

[42] A hymn written by Lucy Rider Myer in 1854 titled, "He Was Not Willing."
[43] Luke 14:26.

by family members who possibly believed they wouldn't need them for a long time anyway.

Besides the heartache of leaving their loved ones behind, there was the hurt of rejection and criticism from others. A common reaction was for people to say, "Leave the Chinese alone. They have their own way of life and religion." But as Leslie Francis stated, "we must realize that our call to China is not to change the system but to work within the limits it imposes."[44] Or, as Geraldine Guiness[45] wrote,

> In China there are hoary systems of philosophy, religion, and culture; we do not seek to add to these. There is an ancient and complex civilisation that it is not ours to supersede with new ideas from the West. One thing, supremely, is lacking; one blessing we wish to bring—the knowledge of a Saviour, and a Saviour's love.

Clifford had another perspective in not wanting to leave the Chinese people to an existence that he perceived to be miserable and hopeless. From an article titled "La Miseré" he described some of the conditions in China:

La Miseré

As we looked out upon this part of the world, we saw what the French term "la miseré." This is the heart of heathendom and we are no longer surrounded by the blessings and comforts which the Gospel message has brought to North America.

All day long the dust-track roads are thronged with countless men, women and children. There are no drains and the sewage runs down open gullies beside the roadway. Flies feed and multiply. They swarm over the meat and the fruit in the open roadside shops. They worry the listless men who sit idly smoking and fanning themselves. They crawl over the faces of others who are asleep. Clusters of idle men crowd the roadsides while others work in the fields twelve hours each day for a pitifully low wage of a few pennies.

Countless babies with gummy eyes and runny noses are everywhere. The older children play in the sun in the dusty roadways as long as it is light, untaught until they start to look for work. They fight, they

---

Francis, p. 41.
Guiness, (1894 II), pp. 390–91.

steal food from the open stalls, and they work for their parents under pressure. They are beaten and have stones thrown at them.

The farming methods are primitive and the land does not fully support the increased population. Many of the people leave for the big towns and cities. Here the pavements are not of gold, but again a few find work and many more stay and hope. The homeless man and his family, who have very little money, find some solution by leasing a rough spot outside the town and building a shelter for themselves.

Shacks are built with anything they can find—mud, bamboo and scraps of wood or stones gathered together. When it rains, which it may do heavily every day for three weeks, it is disastrous. No ramshackle shack is waterproof and to further complicate matters most of them are built directly on the earth. Some of them are washed away by floodwater running down the steep slope. The roads become sluggish mud rivers, the gullies of sewage raging torrents. Disease is uncontrolled. Blindness is unbelievably common. Many faces are permanently disfigured.

There is none of the moral influence of a settled community. There are no churches dotting a peaceful landscape, no Bibles to read, no gleaming hospitals with skilful surgeons and kind nurses, no institutes for the blind, no asylums for the insane, and no homes for the aged, helpless and orphaned. The lepers and beggars wander about, pitiful and wretched and unfed. They live without comfort and without hope.

Such scenes could be multiplied again and again as one peers behind the black curtain of heathenism. Then some people at home will smugly say: "Let the heathen alone. They have their own customs and religion, and they are peaceful and happy."

If you had good news, would you not want to share it? Besides, the missionaries were the same people who brought hygiene and sanitation, hospitals and education—not only for boys but for girls as well. For a long time, girls in China were considered worthless and incapable of learning, thus making it a waste of time and money to try and educate them.

The final criticism, and the one that hurt the most, was, "How could you take a small child to China and put him at risk? Doesn't he deserve better?" The choice was actually quite simple, and was aptly stated by Miriam Dunn in the title of her book, *My Children or the Cross*. She chose the cross. Maybe Clifford and Florence did not consider young Philip their child but God's.

Don't all children belong to Him? But to those not spiritually minded, it would, of course, be considered foolishness.

Once on the mission field, the missionary is separated from their own children when they reach school age, at which point they must attend boarding school, sometimes hundreds to thousands of miles away from the missionary's station. For purposes of the children's education, the CIM had established a boarding school in northeast China, at Chefoo in Shantung Province. In sending her young daughter, Kathyrn, to Chefoo, over two thousand miles away, Isobel Kuhn's cry is the anguish of all missionary mothers:

> I knew that, in one sense, it was giving her up for life. Although our Mission planned that children join their parents when possible for holiday times, one never again could watch them grow from day to day. The parting was excruciating for me, and for hours afterward I could not sit, lie down or do anything but grieve. I poured over all I would miss in putting her to bed at night, her sweet childish ways, the likelihood she would forget me to some extent . . .[46]

Clifford and Florence experienced the same heaviness of heart in leaving Philip but were comforted in the knowledge that he would be safe in God's hands and well cared for by mission staff.

Then there is the constant concern for their children's health alongside a myriad of diseases including diphtheria, scarlet fever, and small pox, with limited Western medicines and medical personnel being long distances away, in the larger centres. And the knowledge that many a missionary's child is buried in China.

With no friends or family close by, the missionary's life is isolated and often lonely. Initially, the missionary is unable to converse with the people. Only with considerable time and study of the language comes any degree of fluency and meaningful contact. External sources of fellowship and friendship are scarce.

Coupled with leaving family is the loss of everything familiar, including the comforts of modern civilization. Isobel Kuhn wrote about this transition:

> Leaving the familiar you are transported to a totally strange environment where, among those of an alien blood, tongue and civilization, you are

---

[46] Kuhn (1997), p. 61.

40

severed from all the associations and influences in which you have been reared. And, when you return to your own country, you feel like a foreigner and alien to it.

To adjust, the missionary must learn to never let anything—family, friends, home or possessions—become so indispensable that, at His call and according to His will, it cannot be given up.

Although the treaty ports[47] like Shanghai were quite modern by Western standards, with paved streets, running water, sanitation facilities, and western homes and amenities, inland China, where Clifford and Florence were to go, was rural and primitive. It was populated by peasants and governed by poverty, with no real comforts or luxuries. In the smaller cities and towns, CIM missionaries typically lived in a compound arranged in a rectangle or U-shape around a courtyard and surrounded by a high wall. Still, there was no plumbing or running water. Toilet facilities consisted of a wooden bucket or an outdoor hole in the ground over which a person would squat.

Huddled closely together, Chinese houses were small in size and had packed mud floors and windows without panes of glass. Some contained rooms for gambling or the smoking of opium. In these rooms addicts would recline on a low sofa with their long pipes resting on the floor and a little bowl of opium at the end. Throughout the cities were small tea houses where a person could refresh himself with a hot cup of tea, and open air markets where food was sold and barbers, dentists, and Chinese doctors plied their trade. There were also a multitude of dogs roaming the streets, scavenging for whatever they could find to eat.

The abject poverty, squalor, filth, and primitive living conditions were appalling, and proved a difficult adjustment for any Westerner. Because human excrement was used for fertilizing crops, bacteria would seep into the lakes and rivers. All drinking water had to be boiled, fruit peeled, and vegetables bleached. Any domestic worker had to be educated in hygiene practices and watched closely, as a cloth used to wash a floor or wipe a nose might also be used as a dish towel. Even when back in Canada Clifford regimentally followed the sanitary practices learned in China and, when at a restaurant, he would scrupulously clean his cutlery before eating.

---

47 Through various wars with China, the European powers were able to establish free ports for themselves for purposes of commerce and trade.

Some of the missionaries, like Isobel Kuhn, were exposed to the most primitive of conditions while working among the mountain tribespeople. In her book *In the Arena*, she wrote:

> The China Inland Mission, true to its name, reached out to the unworked interior of that great land, where by far the great majority of unevangelized Chinese were country peasants, poor people who toil and labour in mud hovels and know nothing of the luxuries of hot baths with soap, or frequent change to clean clothing. I had to learn that it costs money to be clean; I had always taken cleanliness for granted . . .
>
> As in all eastern lands . . . these toiling people had vermin on their persons, in their homes, and in the dust of their mud floors. Fleas jumped on me from those floors and nibbled joyfully. . . . Sitting close to a country woman, I was likely to carry away a louse. And when asked to spend a night in these homes, bedbugs walked out in regiment upon me, not to speak of the air force—flies and mosquitoes.[48]

Another adjustment for the missionary was the loss of privacy, personal space, and peace and quiet. Within 125 miles of Shanghai lived almost as many people as in the whole of Canada; the interior was also heavily populated. They were called the teeming masses: an overwhelming crush of humanity constantly pushing, pressing, shoving, and touching. The Chinese did not understand the Westerner's need for privacy. Most rural peasant families lived, ate, and slept in one room, everyone together. The Chinese were curious about the foreigners living among them. They wanted to examine and touch everything from their faces and hair to their clothes and belongings. Their logic was, if a person was not doing anything wrong, then there was no reason to hide from scrutiny.

In China, there was no such thing as peace and quiet, something which Clifford found particularly disconcerting. There was always noise—the noise of hawkers pedalling their wares; the chanting of coolies[49] carting their loads along the street; the constant hum of people chattering; and the ringing of the temple bells, slow and monotonous, ring after ring after ring. Their tolling meant that tormented souls in the afterlife were experiencing relief. It was

---

[48] Kuhn (1997), p. 37.
[49] A Chinese labourer who transports goods or people using various wheeled conveyances.

believed that the vibrations of the bell drove the demons temporarily insane, so that, for a while at least, they could not continue their torturous actions.

Although Clifford was dismayed by the poverty he saw in China, he was also concerned with the spiritual risks of prosperity. In the New Testament, Matthew[50] talks about a young man approaching Jesus and asking how he might attain eternal life.

> Jesus said unto him, "If thou wilt be perfect, go and sell that thou hast, and give to the poor, and thou shalt have treasure in heaven: and come and follow me."
>
> But when the young man heard that saying, he went away sorrowful: for he had great possessions.
>
> Then said Jesus unto his disciples, "Verily I say unto you, That a rich man shall hardly enter into the kingdom of heaven."
>
> And again I say unto you, "It is easier for a camel to go through the eye of a needle, than for a rich man to enter the kingdom of God."

In a similar vein, Clifford wrote the narrative of a young Chinese man caught in the trap of prosperity.

The Three Pictures

A few years ago in the city of Sinyuin, Chekiang Province, China, a poor beggar found his way to the small Christian chapel in that city. He had been a beggar for many years. He had no clothes but the dirty strips he had gathered from the garbage piles of the city and tied as best he could in loose folds about his thin, emaciated body. His body was full of sores and filth and his hair had been eaten away by what we call "lah-tji teo", "the disease of white flakes", which is the beginning of the form of leprosy all too common among the many beggars of the East.

As this poor human derelict stood leaning on his staff at the door of the Christian chapel listening to the simple message of Christ and His love, he realized a sense of his sin and a need for a Saviour. He then and there resolved in his heart to be a follower of the Lord and from that day on regularly attended the Gospel meetings. One day coming into the mission compound in his rags, it was decided to get a picture of him, not so much to get a picture of his rags but to catch the new glow which had come to his very face.

---

[50] Matthew 19:21–24.

Then the evangelist and some of the Christians in pity for him decided to take him and get him cleaned up by introducing him to some soap and water, and then give him some much-needed medical attention and purchase for him some new garments. A few days later the Christians gave him some money to open a small stall on the main street where he was able to sell odds and ends of things such as shoe laces, buttons, matches, and so on. He was very happy. He regularly attended the Sunday services each Sunday, learned to read and write and, in a few years time, became one of the leaders in that church.

God blessed him in his business which grew and expanded. He early resolved that he as a Christian would give to the Lord's work 10 out of every 100 which he made. Now dressed in presentable garments he had a picture taken of himself and given to the local church in appreciation of their love for him and interest in him. His business increased each year. The first year it was something over a hundred dollars, then it increased to 200, then 400, then 600, 700, and in a few years with care and thrift and determination it amounted to 1,000 Mexican silver dollars.

Prior to this he had regularly paid his tithe—1/10th on everything he earned. But the year he earned the $1,000 he hesitated. He looked at his tithe—$100 out of the thousand—surely, this was too much to give and he didn't give it that year. But (listen) from that time on he began to go downhill—materially and spiritually. He began to miss his Sunday worship with the little Christian group which had befriended him. Soon he began to associate with worldly company, and began gambling, the besotting sin of most Chinese. Then, one day surrounded by his worldly companions, he lost all at the gambling table—all his earnings, even the earnings of the past years. His business and his business connections, even the clothes which he possessed, were all swept away in that one day. What sorrows now!

Nothing was left for him to do but to go back to the old job of begging which he had done for so many many years. In a few months time he was again clothed in his rags. Coming to the mission compound one day, the missionary was able to get a third picture of him, a picture showing him again in the tattered rags, with the staff and a little tin begging pan in his outstretched hands. Everything gone and back to the same old place and the same old condition.

If you went this morning to the city of Sinyuin, you would very likely see this man slowly traversing the streets of that city in search of food and help. And if you would ask the missionary at the mission station in that city, he could show you the three snapshots of which he told me. The first, showing what Tan was before the missionaries found him, the second one showing Tan at the height of his prosperity in his silk gown and shiny silk shoes, and then a third picture of Tan again a beggar at the doorway asking for alms. O the deceitfulness of prosperity!

X

China: 1930s

The times were troubled and troubling.

Clifford and his young family entered a China convulsed with civil war. In 1928, Chiang Kai-shek and his party, the Kuomintang, assumed power over southern China with the aim of uniting the country as a sovereign nation. To do so, he needed to wrest power from the warlords who controlled the rest of China. Earlier, in 1920, the Communist Party had been formed, supported by Russia. It, too, wanted a unified China with one central government, but under Communist rule. Continuous skirmishes and wars were fought between the two factions.

Although Chiang Kai-shek was receptive to the West and foreign missionaries, the Chinese Communist Party, which was formulated along Soviet-Marxist lines, was not. It viewed religion as the opiate or panacea of the masses and classified missionaries as Imperialist spies and enemies of the people. At various times they persecuted the Chinese Christians and foreign missionaries, by kidnapping and holding them for ransom or by killing them. If held for ransom, the extorted monies were used to further the Communist cause and provide support for their members.[51]

In 1929, Esther Nordlund,[52] a missionary with the Evangelical Church in the province of Hupeh, was kidnapped by Communist forces along with two other missionaries and a Chinese medical doctor. They were held for ransom for seven days but were released through the intercession of the captured doctor.

---

[51] Rich Chinese landowners were also taken hostage and their relatives required to pay large sums of money for their release. Despite the ransom being paid, the landowner was usually killed anyway.

[52] Esther was later killed in 1948 by Communist bandits while travelling by bus with two co-workers. None of the Chinese passengers were harmed. Esther was just 51 years of age.

Then, on October 1, 1934, just two weeks before the Paulsons arrived in China, communist soldiers captured five CIM missionaries—Alfred and Rose Bosshardt, Arnolis and Rhoda Hayman along with their two young children, and another missionary, Grace Emblen. Although the wives and children were soon released, the three remaining missionaries were forced to march with communist soldiers fleeing their main base in Kiangsi Province, intending to set up a new base in Shansi Province some six thousand miles away. This famous communist trek became known as the "Long March." An estimated one hundred thousand men and women began the march but only ten thousand survived. Along the way, Grace managed to escape when she stopped to rest and the communist troops moved on without her. Alfred and Arnolis remained on the march. During their ordeal, the men were often deprived of food or relegated to eating mouldy rice; they were constantly beaten, threatened with death, and forced to march long distances, sometimes up to forty miles a day over rugged terrain and for as long as thirty-six hours. They were paraded through villages along the way, where they were spat on and pummelled by the villagers.

Alfred and Arnolis dealt with their captivity by praying for their captors, singing hymns, reciting Bible verses, and counting their blessings. They would also recall the events of the day for which they were grateful and praise God for the strength to carry on. At night, Alfred, who had learned to crochet as a child, crocheted hats, mittens, and socks for the communist guards.

After 2,500 miles of travel and 413 days of captivity, Arnolis was released when a friend of the mission paid a ransom of ten thousand silver dollars. Although it was paid for the release of both men, the communists reneged on their deal and released only Arnolis. By then, he was unable to walk and weighed barely one hundred pounds.[53]

Six months later, after 560 days in captivity, Alfred was released. He was deathly ill and required complete bed rest for eleven weeks before he was even close to recovery.[54] But he was alive, and he was far more fortunate than

---

[53] Later, Arnolis faced more trials when his children, who had been attending school at Chefoo with Philip, were interned by the Japanese at Weishien.

[54] When the People's Republic of China was established in 1949, the CIM asked its missionaries to stay in the country despite Communist rule and persecution of their missionaries. However, no such request was made of Alfred given everything he had already gone through. Despite his experiences, Alfred and his family remained.

another missionary, Henry Ferguson, who was taken by the Communists in 1933. He was never heard from again.

John and Betty Stam, CIM missionaries, were captured by communist forces on December 6, 1934, in the small village of Tsingteh, just north of Hwaining, where the Paulsons were attending language school. The Stams were held for ransom, but before the ransom letter could be delivered, they were marched twelve miles across the mountains to Maio Sheo, where they were paraded through town in their undergarments before being beheaded. John was twenty-seven years old, Betty twenty-eight.

Who can know the purpose in the martyrdom of these two fine young people? Maybe it was to strengthen believers, maybe it was a call to others to serve. Indeed, in a memorial service for the Stams held at Moody Bible Institute, seven hundred students stood up to consecrate their lives to missionary service.

Another CIM couple, the Porteouses, were captured by communist bandits and held for a number of months. When the decision was made to execute them, they were taken to a lonely spot on top of a hill. As the executioner removed his sword from its shoulder strap, Mr. Porteous felt a certain peace with God, and he and his wife began to sing:

Face to face with Christ, my Saviour,
Face to face—what will it be,
When with rapture I behold Him,
Jesus Christ who died for me?

Face to face I shall behold Him,
Far beyond the starry sky;
Face to face in all His glory
I shall see Him by and by![55]

As they were singing, the bandit slowly shouldered his sword. Sometime later the couple was released.

Besides peril from roving bands of communists, China was rife with bandits who would waylay and rob travellers or raid cities and villages for food, monies, and goods. For protection, cities were surrounded by high,

[55] Hymn by Carrie E. Breck titled, *Face to Face*.

wide walls for sentries to walk around and large gates that were locked at night. Violence was just a normal part of life.

Despite all the danger, Clifford and Florence walked in faith into the land in which God had called them to serve.

> . . . neither count I my life dear unto myself, so that I might finish my course with joy, and the ministry, which I have received of the Lord Jesus, to testify the gospel of the grace of God. (Acts 20:24)

XI

Language Studies

Oh Lord, my God,
When I in awesome wonder,
Consider all the worlds Thy hands have made;

I see the stars,
I hear the rolling thunder,
Thy power throughout the universe displayed.[56]

From Shanghai, the young family travelled three hundred miles west by steamer along the Yangtze River, to Hwaining, located in the southeast part of Anhwei Province. When Clifford first saw the Yangtze, he was captivated by the majesty of it and often talked about it in his speaking engagements and writings:

> Starting as a tiny trickle in the mountains of the Tibetan border, the Yangtze River becomes increasingly deeper and wider as it winds its way through central China for 3,000 miles to the Yellow Sea. As it moves along, other streams and rivers flow into it while others flow out, creating large tributaries along its route. It is the largest waterway in China and the fifth largest in the world. At its mouth it is 60 miles wide; 700 miles of it are navigable, making it possible for large ships to sail up it. Other than its yellow muddy colour, it is an awe-inspiring sight.[57]

To Clifford it was a supreme example of God's creation.

Anhwei was a picturesque province, with green hills, mountains, and an abundance of rivers and streams. Covering the sides of the hills were terraces

---

[56] One of Clifford's favourite hymns, *How Great Thou Art*, written by Carl Boberg to a Swedish folk melody.
[57] Written by Clifford and adapted by M. J. Paulson.

of rice paddies. Irrigation was provided by collecting water from the upper reaches of the mountain streams and siphoning it down the hillsides. As the water travelled down from terrace to terrace, it came to rest in small rivers hundreds of feet below.

Clifford and Florence thoroughly enjoyed the scenery along the river. As their steamer approached the city, a smaller boat came out from the shore and travelled alongside it. Passengers and baggage were transferred without either boat stopping. Once everything was unloaded, the small boat proceeded to shore where the passengers alighted. From there, Clifford and Florence carried on to the language school where they were to study the Chinese language and culture before venturing on to their first posting. Hwaining was specifically chosen for language training as the dialect there was similar to the Chinese spoken throughout most of the country.

A term at language school usually lasted eight or nine months. The CIM expected their missionaries to be conversant in Chinese, both written and spoken, and acclimatized to their food and social customs before working among them. The male missionaries were trained at the Hwaining language school while the female missionaries went to Yangchow, near Shanghai. However, because Clifford was married, Florence attended school with him. She was the only female missionary candidate there, and Philip the only white child.

The days at language school were spent learning to read, write, and speak Chinese—studying the vocabulary, pronunciation and tone, and becoming acquainted with the Chinese culture and diet. Chinese meals were served weekly as a means of introducing the candidates to the different types of food and how they tasted. Whatever time was left was given over to prayer, church services, and various recreational activities including walks around the city and the surrounding countryside.

In China there are two forms of the language, Mandarin and Cantonese, along with various dialects for each. Mandarin was the official language, used by scholars and government officials, and was spoken throughout most of mainland China whereas Cantonese was predominant in southern China. Mandarin has four tones, Cantonese six.

Chinese is one of the world's most difficult languages to learn, both in the reading and speaking of it. Instead of an alphabet from which words are formed, written Chinese uses thousands of pictorial symbols or "characters."

Each symbol denotes a word and must be learned on its own, as well as in combination with others to form different words. In illustration, the symbols for sun and moon when placed together mean "brightness." Making it even more difficult, each character can be used as a noun, verb, adjective, or adverb, its function dependent on its placement with other symbols. To be literate, a person must be able to read and write at least three thousand symbols; to enjoy a scholarly book, a reader must know several thousand more. Learning to write Chinese is also difficult and is a feat of both memory and graphic skill. Each character is composed of a number of strokes, some upwards of eighteen.

Then there is spoken Mandarin. It is tonal, with four pitched tones for each word. As tone varies, so does meaning. In illustration, the word "ma" could mean mother, hemp, horse, or scold, each dependant on the tone used. Sounds may also have different meanings. For example, the sound "i" has seventy-five distinct meanings, from salt to righteousness to eye, depending on which tone is used and how it is combined with other symbols. Even after months of language study candidates are likely to make several faux pas, such as addressing the "honourable" audience as "devil" people or preaching a sermon on the subject of Noah's dog.

In learning the language, Clifford came to believe that China had been exposed to Christianity early in its history. He based his belief on the Chinese script for boat, which is comprised of three characters—vessel, the number eight, and people. Clifford felt that this combination of symbols referred to Noah's ark and the eight people in it.

boat

舟 八 口

vessel   eight   people

After completing their language studies, the Paulsons had to pass the prescribed language examinations before they would be considered sufficiently proficient to function independently. Thereafter their fluency would be perfected under private tutelage.

Besides study of the language, language school also provided an opportunity for mission leaders to assess the character and abilities of each prospective missionary. These assessments determined where each candidate might best be placed in the mission field, and with whom.

XII

Acclimatization: Diet

(In a trance, Peter) saw heaven opened, and a certain vessel descending unto him . . .

Wherein were all manner of fourfooted beasts of the earth, and wild beasts, and creeping things, and fowls of the air.

And there came a voice to him, Rise, Peter; kill and eat.

But Peter said, Not so, Lord; for I have never eaten any thing that is common or unclean.

And the voice spake unto him again the second time, What God hath cleansed, that call not thou common.

(ACTS 10:11–15)

Clifford and Florence enjoyed their Chinese meals both at language school and later, when working in their own mission station. Ordinary Chinese fare was usually a bowl of rice with a few shreds of local vegetables or yam and maybe a few scraps of chicken or pork. There was in-season fruit, as well as eggs and peanuts, and always steaming hot cups of tea. On special occasions, such as birthdays and Christian holidays, Florence might have asked for a whole chicken to be butchered.

Most foods had to be eaten within a day or two of purchase as they spoiled quickly in the heat. The only way of preserving them for any length of time was to put them down a well to keep them cool. Fresh produce was bought daily at open air stalls in markets. Prepared foods could be purchased from vendors who cooked small dumplings or various delicacies in a boiling pot of water or a metal frying pan sitting atop a charcoal fire. However, certain Western commodities were unattainable altogether, including coffee, milk, and refined sugar. Only coarse raw brown sugar extracted from sugar cane was available.

Totally different fare was served at Chinese feasts, to which Clifford and Florence were often invited. Delicacies, which were not readily available at other times, would grace the menu—one hundred-year-old eggs,[58] whole fish cooked with the head and entrails, gobs of boiled fat, and bird's nest soup. Fish eyes were a particular delicacy and, when presented for a guest's consumption, were considered a great honour.

Florence was not particularly fond of some delicacies, apart from fish cooked in brown sugar. At a feast, fish eyes were often served to Clifford. He, in turn, would mischievously present them to Florence as a further sign of honour and respect for her. Of course, Florence would be dismayed but graciously have to accept. Then, when no one was looking, she would surreptitiously drop them to the floor. The one problem was the ever-present dogs hovering nearby or under the table anxiously waiting for whatever scraps of food might fall. When Florence discarded the honoured morsel, there was a mad scramble for it, with the dogs growling and fighting, the table being upended and dishes flying everywhere.

Bird's nest soup was a bit harder to discard and generally had to be eaten, slurped loudly to show one's appreciation. The soup was made from a certain bird's vomit, which the bird used to line her nest. When trying to eat the slimy, stringy white substance, one part of it would start to slip down the throat while the rest would stay in one's mouth as desperate attempts were made to swallow all of it.

[58] A one hundred-year-old egg is not, as its name suggests, a hundred years old. It is a preserved chicken or duck egg. First the egg is soaked in a mixture of salt, lime, and ash, then rolled in mud, wrapped in rice husks, and buried for a number of weeks. The process turns the egg whites to a translucent, jelly-like amber, and the yolks to dark green or slightly black. When eaten, the texture of the egg is much like a hardboiled egg, although the taste is pungent like ripe blue cheese, with a faint hint of ammonia.

XIII

China: Religions of China

*For thus saith the LORD that created the heavens; God himself that
formed the earth and made it; he hath established it, he created it not
in vain, he formed it to be inhabited: I am the LORD; and there is
none else.*

(ISAIAH 45:18)

As part of their cultural education, Clifford and Florence studied the different
Chinese religions. At that time, China was polytheistic, embracing three major
religions: Confucianism, Taoism, and Buddhism. Most people practised one
or two while others practised all three. There was also a small segment of
Muslims, although they did not proselytize and were simply tolerated.

Confucius was a sixth century Chinese philosopher whose teachings
presented a philosophy of social organization and were not actually a set
of religious beliefs. Confucian thought emphasized a hierarchy of social
relationships of superior and subordinate positions—subject to ruler, wife to
husband, and child to parent.

Each person's behaviour was regulated by a set of social expectations or
duties extending down from emperor to peasant. It was believed that if each
person performed their duty responsibly, society would achieve a state of
harmony and stability. Confucius said,

> When the personal life is cultivated, the family will be regulated; when
> the family is regulated, the state will be in order; and when the state is
> in order, there will be peace throughout the world.[59]

---

[59] Scott, p. 95.

Duty was all-important, and the most important duties were loyalty and obedience. These were the underpinnings of Chinese culture and social structure. Individual rights and freedoms did not matter.

Through Mencius, Confucius's disciple, came the thought that human nature was basically good and that man was born with an innate moral sense. This contrasted with Christianity's focus on the concepts of personal sin and a moral God. According to Confucian thinking, the rulers and upper class were to be a moral example to the people. The emperor was called the Son of Heaven and was expected to care for the welfare of his citizens. If there was any evil in society, it was a result of immoral leaders and the failure to order society along the proper lines of authority. Through education, personal efforts at self-cultivation, and emulating good role models, man could be led along the right path.

Just as the natural universe was orderly, so, too, society was to be organized. Man was considered to be the centre of the universe, not God. Confucianism esteemed age because it denoted wisdom over youth, past over present, authority over creativity, and consistency over change. Education was valued. Being able to read and write were the mark of an educated man, and the act of writing was an art form referred to as calligraphy,[60] which Clifford mastered and practiced throughout his lifetime. Scholars were highly respected because they gave the world thought. This reverence for learning also provided the missionary with a certain amount of esteem, as he was a learned person who could read and write. In contrast, merchants and military men were poorly regarded; merchants were associated with greed and soldiers with violence.

From Confucian veneration of the elderly came the practice of ancestor worship. The Chinese believed that deceased family members lived on in a spirit world and could influence the still-living family. Thus, it was important to show them respect and take care of their needs in order to bring good fortune to the living. Grave sites and ancestral tablets in the home became places of worship. There, incense would be burned and food offered to the spirits of the dead; the thought being that the spirits would partake of the

---

[60] Calligraphy is a stylized form of writing where each Chinese character is formed in a precise manner. It requires a great deal of skill, as the hand has to be held steady with the wrist and the elbow suspended above the table. Then, with complete freedom of movement, each stroke of the brush is made boldly and purposefully.

spiritual essence of these offerings. Besides food, imitation paper money, clothes, houses, sedan chairs, and other essentials, which might be useful in the spirit world, were burned and thereby transported to the spirit world. Only male descendants could be involved in ancestor worship, which made it important for a family to have sons. If there was no son, the spirit of the dead would wander aimlessly, hungry and destitute, and be unable to help the family. If perchance the son became a Christian and no longer participated in the worship of his ancestors, there would be chaos within the family and ensuing animosity.

Taoism, or Daoism as it is sometimes called, is a religious philosophy that emphasizes the importance of achieving harmony in one's life as a means of obtaining peace and spiritual immortality. To attain a harmonious existence, a person must lead a life of simplicity and moderation, humbly accept life's trials and circumstances, and be compassionate toward others. Taoism also entailed a belief in an unseen world of evil spirits or demons and left a legacy of superstitions, sorcery, divination, and astrology.

Evil spirits were believed to lurk everywhere. Often incense was burned or firecrackers lit to drive them away, because evil spirits did not like the smell of gunpowder. Nor did they like the colour red, which was why red banners were placed on houses and in towns. When a house was swept, it was to get rid of evil spirits who might be lurking there, and not for sanitary purposes. Evil spirits did not like light, so electricity in the cities would be turned off during the day but left on at night.

The Chinese believed that evil spirits could only move in straight lines. To keep them at bay, roads, houses, and walls were built crooked. Often a ledge would be placed at the bottom of a door frame, to trip up any evil spirits trying to enter. Doors would be placed on the sides of houses, so that demons would not be able to find their way in. A chimney in a house was never built opposite a neighbour's door. The Chinese word for fire and calamity was "ho," but with a slightly different tone and written form. Because the words sounded similar, it was believed that the fire from the chimney might bring disaster to the other family.

Demons lived everywhere—in trees, rocks, and mountains. Various animistic rituals would be practiced in these locations. Shrines were built to them where people would pray and offer gifts to appease the demons, so they would not bring harm or misfortune to an individual or family. Demons liked to haunt the place where a person had died. Because of this, a dying person at home would be placed outside, on the street. If a Western hospital was close by, the person would be taken there. This practice also allowed the relatives to sue the hospital for funeral expenses or seek an indemnity for "killing" the patient. Sometimes children were given derogatory names in an attempt to deceive the evil spirits into thinking the child was unworthy, just like their name, and not harm them.

Buddhism was the third religion of China. It was first introduced in the sixth century by Buddhist monks and traders travelling from India to China. It views life as an existence of suffering and misery but with the possibility of moving from one existence to another. Moving to a higher form occurs through reincarnations of various life forms, until the highest state is achieved where there is liberation from all suffering. This state is referred to as nirvana or enlightenment. Constant improvement is required to move to a higher state. To do so, a person is to seek self-insight (through meditation), purge themselves of all earthly desires and attachments (through self-denial and sacrifice), pray to Buddha and practice certain rituals, and engage in numerous meritorious acts. It is also possible, however, to revert to a lower form of life as punishment for various nefarious actions or deeds. This is the law of karma.

Buddhists were superstitious and feared dying without their body intact, as a missing body part would prevent reincarnation to a higher life form. When criminals were executed, their heads would be placed in a small cage or on a post separate from the body and out of reach of family members as a further form of punishment. Also, their shoes were removed to prevent the person's spirit from running after and tormenting their executioner.

Buddhist temples existed everywhere in China—in cities, villages, and throughout the countryside where they were usually built on the side of a mountain or near its peak. They were elegant structures, some standing over one hundred feet tall, with a steep winding road leading up to them. They were looked after by Buddhist monks who subsisted on the offerings of worshippers, by begging, or by being paid for their chanting at funerals or various celebrations. Adherents would come to the temple to pray and make requests of Buddha for such things as a good harvest, the birth of a son, or good fortune in the years to come. Incense was burned as a pleasing odour to the Buddha and, sometimes, a monk would beat a large gong to get the

Buddha's attention. Each temple was entered by a massive wooden door at the front, which opened into a large hall. At the far end of the hall would be an enormous wooden statue of Buddha, as tall as thirty feet and seated on a golden throne. In addition to worshipping at the temple, believers would keep a Buddhist shrine in their home, in front of which family members would bow or kneel, repeat various incantations, burn incense, and place plates of food. To a Buddhist, their shrines and temples were holy. Any sacrilege was a great offence.

Dr. Eleanor Chesnut, a medical missionary with the American Presbyterian Board, experienced the wrath of the Buddhist community when their idol shrine was violated. In 1905, while Dr. Chesnut was working at a hospital in Kwangsi province, the Chinese were busy celebrating the Buddhist holiday of Ta Tsin. Dr. Machle, head of the mission station, insisted that a shed, which was on hospital grounds but was being used for idol worship during the festival, be removed.

> Local officials consented to remove it, but at the objection of some of the citizens who were offended that their culture had been violated. These in turn were able to incite a menacing mob to march on the mission property. Eleanor, sensing the danger, slipped away from the hospital to plead to the local authorities for help. She could have escaped harm altogether by staying where she was, but instead rushed back to assist her coworkers.
>
> Meanwhile the mob had rushed onto the hospital premises. They found Dr. Machle, his wife and child, and Reverend and Mrs. John Peale trying to flee. The Peales were new missionaries who had just arrived the previous day. The half-crazed crowd chased down the fleeing missionaries and killed all five next to the river in front of a Buddhist temple. They had just finished the killing when Eleanor returned, rushing to help them.
>
> Seizing her, the mob pushed her down the temple steps to the foot of a large tree. She freed herself and sat down on a mound to see what they would do. At that moment she noticed a little boy in the crowd with an ugly gash on his head incurred by the frenzied throng. In the midst of the mayhem she called him over, tore off the hem of her dress, and bound his wound "with skilled, kind fingers that did not tremble," as a witness would later report. This final act of kindness did nothing to placate the incensed mob.

They waited until she was through, then converged on her again. Four ruffians rushed upon her, dragged her down the steep bank and threw her into the river. Then one jumped into the water and stabbed her three times (with a pitchfork)—once in the neck, once in the chest, and once in the abdomen. About ten minutes later they brought her body to shore.[61]

---

[61] Newell, pp. 47–48.

XIV

China: Social Structure, Norms, and Etiquette

For though I be free from all men, yet have I made myself servant unto all, that I might gain the more . . . .

To the weak became I as weak: I am made all things to all men that I might by all means save some.

(I Corinthians 9:19, 22)

Besides learning the Chinese language and becoming conversant in it, Clifford and Florence needed to understand Chinese norms and customs if they were to work effectively in their new homeland. When Hudson Taylor first established the mission, he emphasized the importance of conformity to the Chinese people in three things: language, dress, and customs—provided they did not conflict with biblical principles. This made it easier for the missionary to settle in their midst, and to communicate freely with and be accepted by them. In truth, the Chinese were always impressed and pleased that a foreigner cared enough and spent the time to learn their language. As to dress, Clifford continued to wear Western clothes but did go by his Chinese name, Bao Li-sheng, whereas Florence and the children adopted native attire. Operating within local customs was also important so as not to offend the Chinese. Mistakes of propriety are always easy to make but very difficult to repair, and have made the ministry of a number of missionaries ineffective.

The basic social structure in China was embodied in the family unit headed by the father and eldest son. All female family members were subservient to them. The purpose of marriage was to produce sons whose filial duty was to look after his parents when they were old, and even when they died to look after their spirits in the afterlife. Marriages were usually arranged through an elderly woman who ensured a harmonious match between the two families with respect to wealth, status, and background. Once married, or even betrothed, the girl served in her in-laws' home under the direct rule of the mother-in-law. Virtually she was a servant to the whole family—her husband, his siblings, and his parents.

Girls were considered as belonging to someone else and just another mouth to feed until they became part of their husband's family. They were of no value and were often referred to as a "commodity-on-which-money-has-been-lost." It was considered a waste of money to educate and teach them to read and write; and pointless too, as it was believed they were not capable of learning anyway. Only with the arrival of the missionary came the education of Chinese women.

Sometimes, when a family was poor or had had "too many" female children, a girl would be sold, abandoned, or even drowned at birth. Most missionaries had the experience of a newborn infant being dropped at their doorstep. Later, during the Paulsons' missionary service, their young son Keith heard a baby crying outside the compound. He informed Florence, who retrieved the infant and cared for her until a suitable Chinese family was found to take her in on a permanent basis. Numerous other discarded children were rescued by missionaries and placed in orphanages established by various Protestant and Catholic missions.

One well-known missionary involved in the rescue of these children was Gladys Aylward. Although Gladys had been rejected as a mission candidate by the CIM because of her limited education, she refused to be dissuaded from her calling to serve the Lord in China. By living frugally and saving the money she'd gained working as a maid in London, she eventually had the fare for a train ticket. Travelling overland through Europe and Siberia, she finally reached northern China. During her ministry there in the 1930s, she became involved in rescuing unwanted children, housing and feeding them in her mission compound. When the Japanese Army took over that part of the country, she remained but eventually had to flee when a price was put on her head by the Japanese High Command. Leaving Yangcheng, she set out on foot for Shensi in Free China, taking with her over a hundred children ranging in age from three to sixteen years. The journey took a month, with the unseemly group walking almost three hundred miles over several mountain ranges and crossing the Yellow River. During their long and arduous journey, Gladys kept the children occupied by having them sing various hymns, including *Count Your Blessings*:

When upon life's billows
You are tempest tossed,
When you are discouraged
Thinking all is lost,

Count your many blessings
Name them one by one,
And it will surprise you
What the Lord hath done.[62]

Although the Paulsons never crossed paths with Gladys while in China, they did meet her later in life, when she visited Canada.

In China women had no authority of their own. As a child, a girl had to be obedient to her father; when married, to her husband; and when widowed, to her eldest son. If a woman was divorced and forced to leave her husband's home, she lost any remnant of respectability and all means of support. Not only was her physical well-being in jeopardy but her afterlife as well, as there would be no one to provide for her when she entered the spirit world.

Because of the inferior position of women in Chinese society, female missionaries were under particular scrutiny and had to behave with scrupulous decorum. There could be no public displays of affection with their husbands, and they needed to dutifully walk behind them when out in public. To do otherwise would be immoral.

Politeness was all important. Other people were always addressed as superior, using such terms as honourable and worthy, whereas any self-reference was to be humble and self-effacing. A visitor in a Chinese home was routinely offered a cup of tea and, if invited to a meal, the best food the family could afford and a seat of honour at the table.

In business dealings, whether it was the purchase of a piece of land or a building, the first offer was always refused. There would be reciprocal negotiations until a final price was reached. All transactions were prolonged and ponderous. Haggling in the marketplace was expected. When an important matter needed to be discussed, it was never presented in a forward

---

62 Written by Johnson Oatman Jr. in 1897.

manner. First, four or five unrelated matters would be introduced before the actual concern was presented. Nothing was ever addressed plainly or directly.

It was also considered good manners to refuse a gift when first offered. To accept immediately was considered avarice, but to refuse altogether was extremely rude. The polite response was to refuse several times before accepting the gift. In her book *Jan Wong's China*, Ms. Wong described the protocol prescribed when she was offered a peeled apple that had been placed on "a dirt-encrusted, fly-blown coffee table."

> To refuse was out of the question. Actually, proper Chinese etiquette demanded I pretend to refuse it. Polite guests never accepted something the first time it was offered. Or the second. The third time was borderline okay. But you always accepted in the end. The young assistant thought I had exquisite manners when I kept refusing to eat her apples. Eventually, like every good guest, I acquiesced. As I munched away, I closed my eyes, and prayed to the god of the intestinal tract. (p. 41)

In itself, outright lying was not considered unethical or impolite. If someone did not want to see a visitor, the visitor would be informed that the person was not at home. The only problem was that the visit could only be postponed, as courtesy demanded a return visit be made. Losing face was a major issue for the Chinese. If a person was made to look bad or openly disrespected, he was said to have "lost face." If the offence was serious enough, the offended person might even commit suicide. In China, suicide was considered an acceptable and honourable way to die, especially if a person had brought shame or dishonour to themselves or their family.

Colours were also important. White was associated with death, yet it was the colour most often worn by missionaries. In turn, red was the colour of happiness and was used at weddings, while to the Westerner, it was synonymous with a wanton woman.

XV

Posting to Kweiki

So shall my word be that goeth forth out of my mouth: it shall not
return unto me void, but it shall accomplish that which I please,
and it shall prosper in the thing whereto I sent it.

(ISAIAH 55:11)

By the spring of 1935, Clifford and Florence, having completed their formal language training, were posted to Kweiki, in the northern part of Kiangsi province. Situated approximately 155 miles south of Hwaining, Kweiki was a central town nestled on the Kwangsin River. Along the river were various other towns, with the whole area known as the Kwangsin River basin. It was where the Paulsons would do most of their missionary service. The mission's policy was to place one or two of their missionaries in a major town and have them cover that station as well as the surrounding countryside and nearby villages, referred to as outstations. There, the young couple continued their Chinese Bible and language studies under private tutelage.

Kiangsi is an exceptionally beautiful province stretching from Poyang Lake in the north to the Kweilin Mountains in the south. Most of the province is mountainous, interspersed with numerous rivers and waterways. Poyang Lake empties into the Yangtze River, which forms part of the northern border of Kiangsi. Numerous rivers flow out of the lake in all directions, reaching almost every city in the province and making travel by boat both economical and efficient.

The Kwangsin River flows from the southeast corner of Poyang Lake and, after some distance, enters the Kwangsin River basin. It is an area surrounded by hills, where vegetables, rice, and tea are grown, not only in the valley but also in terraces across the hillsides. It has a humid subtropical climate with cool, damp winters and excessively hot summers. In the 1880s, a number of CIM female missionaries had opened the area to Christian work.

By this time, Clifford was relatively conversant in the Chinese language, although technically speaking, he was still not proficient in it. Complete proficiency would take another year or two and would require him to speak the language fluently, as well as read the Bible in Chinese and communicate it effectively.

Transcribing Bible stories and their concepts for Chinese comprehension was difficult. The Chinese had never heard of prophets and had no idea where the biblical lands were. In the central and southern parts of China, many had never seen sheep, and where there were sheep, they were considered the lowest form of animal and shepherds the basest of men. In the Bible, the dragon is a symbol for Satan, whereas the Chinese view the dragon as a symbol of intelligence, beneficence, and power. The Chinese considered blood filthy, so when a Christian orated about being "washed in the blood of the Lamb," he was being more than revolting; he was being obscene. Then there were references that ran totally counter to Chinese customs. The Bible spoke of the right side as the place or seat of honour; however, in China, the left side was the favoured seating position. Similarly, the Chinese did not like water and did not view bathing as important, so practices like baptism and the washing of feet were considered very strange.

The idea of sin was a foreign concept. There was no Chinese word for sin, with the closest approximation being a crime. This proved a stumbling block for the Chinese since they had committed no crime, felt no guilt or need for atonement, and therefore had no need of a saviour. Along Confucianist lines of thinking, man was basically good and had control over his own destiny. Evil pertained to spirits who dwelt everywhere and schemed to interfere with a person's good fortunes. The Chinese did, however, understand the mediational role of Christ's work of redemption, given their use of middlemen in any business transaction.

Although Confucianism was the underpinning of the Chinese social system, Buddhism was the major religion. As a religion, Buddhism focused on works and rituals while Christianity focused on faith. Buddhism had no god whereas Christianity held to a belief in the one God who created the universe and everything in it, including mankind.

Despite the religious differences, the Chinese people, for the most part, were receptive to Christian teachings. Their tolerance for different religions and philosophies was likely a result of the Confucian respect for education. And though they referred to missionaries and other white people as "yang kuei tsz" or foreign devils, they had rather endearing expressions for the Bible and God. The word "Happy Sound" or "Books of the Happy Sound" referred to the Bible, and "Venerable Heavenly Ruler" was a common term for God, especially among non-Christians.

Although Clifford at the time was a fledgling preacher, he also happened to be a gifted artist. Using his artistic talents along with his limited Chinese, he was able to succinctly convey the gospel's message. First he would put a large sheet of white paper on a stand and, while talking, illustrate in picture form his message. Another fellow missionary, Vincent Crossett, used a different but very innovative strategy.

> Taking a large colored poster, he hung it on the wall in front of the chapel and endeavored to tell the passers-by the meaning of the picture. Most of the people had no idea what he was saying and a majority of them could not read. As he spoke, he watched to see if anyone looked intelligent enough to get a little of the meaning and after he finished speaking, nodded to the most-interested-looking person and asked, "Do you understand what I am saying?" If he replied in the affirmative, (Vincent) said "Then will you please stand up here in front and tell these people what I have been trying to say?" The man would get up and preach to the people, though he himself had heard the gospel for the first time only a few minutes before.[63]

And thus the gospel was preached!

In her Bible teachings, Florence used object lessons and flannelgraph presentations. While relaying a particular Bible story, she would illustrate it by attaching related cardboard characters and props to a flannel sheet. Other times, when presenting the subject of salvation, she would:

> ... use the object lesson of the four boxes: First, a black box representing our sinful hearts; then a red box, representing the shed Blood of Jesus Christ. The black box fits inside the red one, illustrating the covering

---

[63] Crossett, pp. 1–2.

power of the Blood of our Lord. The red box fits into a white one which represents a heart washed white as snow. A black mark is made on the white box but quickly erased to show that if we who have put our trust in Christ and confess our sins, He is faithful and just to forgive our sins and cleanse us from all unrighteousness. These all fit into a yellow box which tells of the joy of heaven.[64]

At the station in Kweiki, Clifford held regular church services in the mission chapel and preached in the village squares and markets, and in neighbouring towns. Florence worked primarily with women and children. She held Bible classes, visited and preached in their homes, and taught them to read, as most, if not all, were illiterate.

In order to do her missionary work, Florence, like other female missionaries, required local servants to do the cooking and housekeeping, and to help with the care of the children. Otherwise the work would have been all-consuming. In addition to the basic chores, food had to be bought daily at the market; water had to be hauled from the well; salt and sugar, which were sold in stone-like lumps, had to be granulated by hand; rice had to be pounded to make a type of flour; and waste had to be removed. Fortunately, hired labour was more than affordable.

The two tasks left for her were the decision-making and supervision of the servants. Supervision was most important, as detailed by Isobel Kuhn:

> You must teach him not to throw egg-shells behind the stove, that the sweepings of the kitchen floor will be discovered if pushed behind the door, not to throw dirty dishwater on the floor . . . and not to wipe the dirt off his hands on the wall. (p. 277)

As part of the ministry, Florence often went out into the community to hand out tracts. Some people could read, but most could not and would, in all certainty, find someone to read it to them—Confucian reverence for education and the written word dictated so. Tracts were also used to open up discussions on morals and ethics—notions in which Confucian scholars were particularly interested.

In a short narrative, Clifford wrote about the importance of the written word.

---

[64] Paulson, p. 84.

C. T. Paulson: Man of War

The Small Slip of Paper

In Shensi lived a man who had become very rich but used his money to buy opium. He went down hill rapidly and soon became an addict. He lost everything he possessed except one little shop. One day as he was walking on the street he found a small piece of paper on which was written two characters, IE SU.

Chinese reverence their own writing and fear that written characters have power and can fall into bad use. Scholars and others pick up all stray papers. Buddhists even engage poor people and beggars to collect any scrap writing. This is done for merit.

Wen looked at these two characters but didn't know what their combined meaning was. He knew "IE" and "SU" separately but . . .

One day as he was sitting up on the counter in his shop, he said to himself, "Why not look up these words in the dictionary." So he got down from the counter, reached up and took his dictionary from the nearby shelf. It was a very early copy of the dictionary but sure enough it showed the combination IE SU and he read what it meant, "According to Western belief, the Saviour of the world."

Wen was struck by this—"the Saviour of the World" and said to himself, "Is it possible that there is a Saviour of the World and I haven't known about it?"

For days he thought about it. He made enquiries from his friends who came to his shop but no one seemed to know a thing about it. No one in the city knew.

Finally one day, a customer friend came into the shop and said, "Say, you have been asking about that IE SU. I have just heard that one of those white foreign devils has come to town and he is preaching and telling about this IE SU."

Wen decided he would go to see the foreigner so he went to his compound and rapped at the gate. The missionary's servant opened the gate and saw the opium sot for everyone in the city knew him. Wen asked "Is the foreign gentleman in who knows about the Saviour of the World? I want to learn about the Saviour of the World. I wonder if He can save me?"

The gatekeeper drove Wen from the door. Wen swallowed his pride for he had lost face and face in China means a good deal—means everything. Wen went back to his shop and thought some more and said to himself "I am going to try again." So he swallowed his pride and went back to the missionary's home. Again the servant opened the gate and saw it was Wen, the opium addict. "Move on. This is no place for you." "But I want to see the foreigner. I want to hear about the Saviour of the World."

"The foreigner is not home. He has gone to the country." (This was a lie, but it was a common thing in China to say when someone's presence is not wanted). "Alright then, I'll sit here and wait." Wen sat down on the doorstep. When the gateman saw that he couldn't shake him off, he went inside and told the foreign missionary. "Sure, call him in."

Wen went in and was taken into the guest hall and put in the seat of honour, something which was rarely done for him in his sunken state, and given a cup of tea. This was a customary courtesy and a sign of hospitality. The two men began to talk.

Usually in China, one begins to speak about four or five other topics before coming to the real point. But this fellow's heart was so full that he began straight off to make enquiries about the Saviour of the World. "I have heard a little about this IE SU. I first saw the name on this little slip of paper—see. Could you tell me more about Him? I wonder if he could save me?"

The missionary took his Bible and began to tell him the story. Before Wen left they knelt together and Wen accepted the Saviour of the World. There was a great change in his life and he was able to break his opium habit. Eventually he became a leader in the local church there in the city.

In time the work grew until there were 40 or more outstations and Wen led hundreds of his fellowmen of that city and surrounding country to Christ.

In disseminating the gospel message, Clifford believed the best messenger was actually the Chinese Christian himself, which he illustrated with this story:

Once a forest was told that a load of axe-heads had come to cut it down. It does not matter in the least, said the forest, for they will never succeed. When, however, it heard that some of its own branches had become handles to the axe-heads, it said, Now we have no longer any chance.[65]

Duncan McRoberts also echoed this theme in his book *While China Bleeds*.

---

[65] Paulson, pp. 42–43.

C. T. Paulson: Man of War

In any land, the natives understand the mind of their own people; they have a thorough knowledge of their background, and are familiar with their manner of reasoning. This is of vital importance . . . . Thus the native can easily win the confidence of his fellow and plainly present the message of Salvation. (pp. 163–64)

XVI

Posting to Hokow

Declare his glory among the heathen; his marvellous works among all nations.

(I Chronicles 16:24)

During the fall of 1936, Clifford and Florence were transferred to Hokow, another major centre east along the Kwangsin River, where Clifford was to be in charge of the mission station. By this time another child had been added to the family—Louise Elaine, born May 31, 1936. Although the infant was initially called Louise, she was later known as Elaine, due to the significant number of missionary children named Louise.

Hokow was a bustling market town of approximately thirty thousand people. At the time, it was the centre for boat and rope making. The houses were single-story structures with mud walls, dirt floors, and tiled roofs. To the north of the city lay a group of irregular, humpy, red rock hills, and to the south was a long stretch of open plain that culminated in the foothills of a long range of high purple mountains extending into the province of Fukien. The mountains were covered with bamboo trees; mountain streams flowed down the sides, converging in small rivers at the base. Rice and tea were grown on the open plain.

The mountains contained thousands of small tribal villages where the Miao lived. They were a people totally unreached by the gospel. The Miao made their living by making paper from bamboo trees. The paper was cut into square sheets, bundled together tightly, and sold in the markets on the plain. The Miao were distinctive in that they bound their heads with a flowery blue-and-white cloth and wore leather shoes, whereas most Chinese shoes were made of cloth.

Hokow still showed signs of the civil war that had raged between communist forces and the Nationalist Army. At various times soldiers would frequent the mission; refugees also arrived from neighbouring parts of the country. Then in July 1937, ten months after the Paulsons' arrival, Japan commenced open war on China even though no war had been declared. Initially the war zone was confined to northeast China, around Peking and Tientsin; however, with each Japanese success, the war spread down the coast rapidly, first to Shanghai and then inland to China's capital city of Nanking. Even though Clifford and Florence were not in an area of direct conflict, the hardships of war began to have an impact on their lives. Supplies and food products became more limited, and telegraph communications and travel were interrupted. To Clifford, the inconveniences of war were of mild concern, and he and Florence continued on with their evangelistic work.

According to CIM policy, missionary service was to be an itinerant ministry. The missionaries were expected to stay at one station just long enough to evangelize the district and help the Chinese Christians set up their own church and gospel outreach. Afterwards they would move on to the next station. Any Chinese dependency was to be discouraged. As Hudson Taylor noted:

> I look on foreign missionaries as the scaffolding round a rising building; the sooner it can be dispensed with the better—or rather, the sooner it can be transferred to other places, to serve the same temporary purpose.[66]

Other than offering spiritual support in the establishment of indigenous churches, the churches themselves were to be totally self-supporting, self-governing and self-propagating. They were to be founded by native Christians and run by local Chinese leaders and elders. Although the missionary might give advice when asked and preach when invited, the Chinese church was to be responsible for conducting its own services and other activities, examining its own candidates for baptism, sending out its own evangelists to the surrounding districts, and disciplining its own members in its own way. It was to financially support its ministers and pay all costs, with no monies provided by the mission or other foreign entities.

---

[66] Taylor (1952b), p. 232.

Later in life, when Clifford returned to Canada and was on the staff at PBI, he taught various courses, one of which was missions. In one of his lectures, he presented the scriptural objectives of missions.

> The general aim, or the aim of missions in its widest scope is to make Christ known as the only Saviour from sin as widely as possible, that is, to preach the gospel in the unreached places. "Ye shall be witnesses unto me . . . unto the uttermost part of the earth" (Acts 1:8) and "they were scattered abroad . . . every where preaching the word" (Acts 8:4). In the early church, the gospel was spread far and wide in accordance with the command of our Lord Jesus Christ, "Go ye into all the world, and preach the gospel to every creature" (Mark 16:15).
>
> On the other hand we see that there is another aspect to the object of missions, that is, to establish a local group or church which will continue to spread the gospel in her own immediate neighbourhood and, in turn, become a missionary centre for reaching out beyond her own borders. Note the churches at Antioch and Thessalonica. This is the conservation of the work of evangelizing, and involves teaching those who are saved. The object of missions then, is not only the evangelizing of individuals or of the masses, but the planting of churches also. The churches then have the responsibility to be missionary minded (Revelation 22:4–5).
>
> All too often, men travel much and preach much but lay no solid foundation or establish anything permanent, leaving unstructured society behind them. It is important not to leave converts isolated, unorganized and wholly ignorant of how to walk in the light of the Gospel.[67]

While living in Hokow, Clifford documented his encounter with one of the local residents, a man named Mr. Liu. He titled the piece *Young Man Who Lost Out*.

> A number of years ago there lived in the city of Hokow in Kiangsi province a promising young fellow, a Chinese, by the name of Liu. He was then only about fifteen years of age. The Gospel had just come for the first time to the city of Hokow. A native Chinese evangelist was already living in the city and now the missionaries had arrived and were preparing to erect a mission station and establish the work there. Young

---

[67] Paraphrased from Clifford's notes.

Liu, unlike a number of the other young people of the city, seemed touched as he came each Sunday to listen to the Gospel story of Christ and his love. He kept coming again and again to stand at the chapel door or sit in the back seat listening to the Gospel being plainly told in his native tongue. With the money he had saved from his meagre earnings he purchased a copy of the Bible in order that he might at his home read more fully about Christ. His regular attendance at the services and his apparent change of attitude about many things such as idolatry and ancestor worship seemed to indicate that God had done a work of grace in his young and tender heart. He was employed for a time in the work of erecting the mission house and an enlarged chapel on the mission compound. Then suddenly the missionaries noticed that he had begun a friendship with a worldly companion, one who was a scoffer and one who had outwardly expressed his hatred and rejection of the Gospel message. Young Liu's zeal began to wane and he began to miss the occasional service, then finally his attendance dropped to once a year at the Christmas Season, then for years and years he never came at all. His friendship with his worldly companion led him into a marriage with a heathen girl and also into business relationships with heathen partners. That was nearly 25 years ago.

Then one day shortly after we had arrived in the city of Hokow, word came to myself and Mr. Ho, the native evangelist, requesting our presence at the southeast suburb of the city to visit someone who was dying. It took us nearly twenty minutes to get to the winding street where the house was to be found. We turned up a squalid side street and stopped at the first house facing East. Glancing inside the door we found that it lead into a large room where an elderly woman sat knitting some old discolored yarn. She said her husband lay dying in the inner court; would we be kind enough to see him as he had been asking to see us. Then she led us through another inner court to a dingy bedroom. Chickens scuttled away as we hurried in and a half-starved mangy dog slunk into the corner.

The bedroom, an inner room, was very, very small and the air in the room seemed exceedingly foul. In the centre of the wall, opposite the door, was a niche with the family idol. In front of this idol, against the wall, was a black lacquered table with a bowl of burning incense. We were asked to sit in the two chairs opposite the idol and were offered cups of lukewarm tea to refresh ourselves after the brisk walk. The many flies which flitted about the dying man and then came to rest on our tea cups took away our desire to take deep satisfying drinks of the tea. The dying man reclined on a hard bamboo bed and a comforter, glossy with the dirt and grease of years, covered his emaciated body. It was Liu, now an old man and now dying of T.B. or what the Chinese call "fei-ping". Beside him on the floor was a pile of ashes to cover and absorb his frequent expectorations. His wife advised us from the doorway that he had of late been unconscious most of the time. Ho suggested we first of all open the one small window before we had prayer and scripture reading. There was no air and very little light in the room.

Going over to the bedside and pushing back the bed curtains, we formally greeted Liu. There he lay (I can see him yet) on his dirty pillow with large haggard eyes and sunken cheeks. His hollow cheeks were nothing more than brown skin pulled tightly over jagged and protruding bones. Noticing that we were near the bed Liu said, "Ngo Szi-ah, Ngo Szi-ah—I am dying—I am dying." "But," he said, "I am resting on the Word of God." We were somewhat surprised at his remark. "How is that," we said, "you began well as a young man. Ni hsiao nien tih tih she heo ken—tsong liao Ie-Su. As a young man you heard the Gospel and began to follow Christ, but where have you been these 25 years? How is it you now say that you are resting on the Word of God?"

"Look," he said in his feeble voice, and then lifting his thin trembling hand he pointed to his old Bible which he had put under his head. He was resting his head upon the old tattered copy of the Scriptures which he had purchased 25 or so years ago when he had first heard the Gospel.

"How sad, Liu," we said, "You know better than that, Liu. You know that the Word of God must be in your heart in order to do you any good. You know that much from your early contacts with the Gospel as a young man. You know, Liu, that there is no use putting the Word of God under your head during your last moments. It must be in your heart, Liu, it must be in your heart."

"Yes, I know," said Liu, "but I have wasted my opportunities. God spoke to me as a young man many many years ago when the Gospel first came to this city but I took another path. Now I am dying and there is nothing more for me, just death itself."

Oh, that Liu would have actually hid God's word in his heart that he might not have sinned against Him!

XVII

Experience with Demonism

And the God of peace shall bruise Satan under your feet . . .
(ROMANS 16:20)

After the Paulsons' postings to Kweiki and Hokow, they moved to Yangchow in 1939, in Kiangsu province. In 1941 they would move back to Kiangsi province, to Shangjao, and then, when their home was bombed by the Japanese that same year, they fled to Yangkow. During their time in China they never experienced a day without war. First, there was the civil war between the communist forces and the Nationalist Army, and then the war with Japan, which was fought entirely on Chinese soil. Finally in 1942, when Japanese forces overran Yangkow, the family fled to Shaowu in Fukien province.

Despite the dark war years, the spiritual darkness of China was worse. Demonism permeated the culture and demon possession was common. This was exemplified in the Boxer Uprising of 1900. The Boxers were a loosely organized society that originated in northern China and whose self-declared mission was to rid the country of foreigners, notably diplomats, missionaries, and their Chinese converts. Prior to their acts of violence, the Boxers engaged in specific rituals in which they prostrated themselves and uttered certain incantations and chants while facing pictures of various deities and invoking their spirits to possess and assist them. A trance followed, characterized by bodily contortions, foam spewing from the mouth, and eyes rolling back in the head, after which they would fall to the ground and then jump up quickly prepared to fight.

When missionaries enter a pagan country, they come face to face with the powers of darkness. Not only are they surrounded by such forces but also they face actual demonic oppression themselves, and certainly demonic opposition to their work. Isobel Kuhn said,

> All missionaries should come to the field with two weapons of warfare against paganism. In our left hand we should wield the weapon of prayer, and in our right the sword of the spirit, which is the word of God.[68]

Similarly, J. O. Fraser learned in his tribal work with the Lisu that "only in a close walk with God and a life of prayer could the powers of darkness be overcome,"[69] for Satan does not easily give up those who have been his for so long.

In a file folder of Clifford's writings, a scrap piece of paper was found on which he'd described an incident of demonic power. Clifford introduced the subject of a young Chinese man who had been converted and was to be baptised but suddenly died. Clifford asked the question, "Why? What happened?" Apparently the man had gone to the home of a heathen friend who asked, "Why have you left the idols?" The young man replied that he no longer believed in them and, reaching down, took some black soot from a pot on the floor and smeared it on the idol's face. The friend was horrified and said, "You will suffer for this. This is a miraculous idol, do you not know?" A few days later the young man died, even though he was not sick or in ill health. Clifford connected his death to the man being "ignorant of Satan" and "not knowing how to combat evil forces."

The young man made three mistakes. First, he underestimated the power of Satan. Lucifer (Satan) was a powerful angel who'd rebelled against God and was thrown out of heaven. Second, he mocked Satan; Satan does not allow himself to be mocked. Even the archangel Michael did not ridicule or scorn Satan when arguing with him, but simply said, "The Lord rebuke thee" (Jude 1:9). And Jesus, when he was tempted by Satan in the wilderness, quoted scripture and merely said, "Get thee hence, Satan" (Matthew 4:1–10). Three, the young man tried to do it with only his own strength. By defying the idol, he was attempting to stand in the place of God. This is pride and was the very reason Lucifer was cast out of Heaven in the first place. In an article written by G. C. Berkouwer, a professor at the Free University of Amsterdam, titled "Satan and the Demons," he noted that Satan "possesses the power to

---

[68] Kuhn (2008), p. 15.
[69] Taylor (2012), p. 122.

overcome us," and that "it is only in God's strength and redemptive power that he can be defeated."[70]

In one of his sermons, Clifford presented the weapons of warfare in dealing with Satanic forces.

The War in Heaven

And there was war in heaven: Michael and his angels fought against the dragon; and the dragon fought and his angels,

And prevailed not; neither was their place found any more in heaven.

And the great dragon was cast out, that old serpent, called the Devil, and Satan, which deceiveth the whole world: he was cast out into the earth, and his angels were cast out with him.

And I heard a loud voice saying in heaven, Now is come salvation, and strength, and the kingdom of our God, and the power of his Christ: for the accuser of our brethren is cast down, which accused them before our God day and night.

And they overcame him by the blood of the Lamb, and by the word of their testimony; and they loved not their lives unto death.

Therefore rejoice, ye heavens, and ye that dwell in them. Woe to the inhabiters of the earth and of the sea! for the devil is come down unto you, having great wrath, because he knoweth that he hath but a short time.

(REVELATION 12:7–12)

In what ways do we successfully thwart the workings of Satan? In viewing the world situation today it almost appears that Satan is triumphant. Godliness, sin and violence abound on every hand. Nations are madly developing weapons which threaten to blot out civilization. Man has the means to liberate the forces which hold atoms together and now has the power to put an end to his own history. The atomic force in the atoms of an ordinary 5 cent coin, if released suddenly, would be powerful enough to blow up most of the city of New York leaving a huge crater hundreds of feet deep. The atomic force in the atoms of the point of a lead pencil if released could run a train around the world twice. In the span of our lifetime we have seen godless communism engulf nearly half the population of the world. On the mission field, we are creeping at a snails pace when we consider the increase of population. Young

---

[70] Henry, pp. 70–75.

men are not applying. There would be real cause for pessimism if it were not for two statements found in verses 8 and 11. Only five words, but: "prevailed not" and "they overcame him."

Notice the remarkably accurate and comprehensive sketch of Satan. Only five words are used to describe him but which aptly reveal his character and power. He is called:

1. **Dragon**—a term which suggests "power." The name is connected with the historical pagan world powers of Egypt (Ezekiel 29:3) and Babylon (Jeremiah 51:34). To the Greek mind, the name conjured up the thought of a great and terrible monster who was malicious, ferocious, cruel and relentless. All you need to do is go to the mission field to see his activity.

2. **Serpent**—a term which suggests "cunning." Other words would be crafty, sly and subtle. He deludes and deceives. He comes as an angel of light but brings false doctrine and lies into the church and among believers. He has three methods of assault upon individuals and nations. His first line of attack is to try and seal off nations and people from hearing the Gospel. He keeps the door closed as was true in China and Japan for centuries. If this scheme fails, he makes a direct attack upon Christians and churches. When the doors are pried open, then he sends in false teachers with the true ones. Japan was flooded early with liberals and modernists following World War II.

3. **Devil**—meaning "slanderer," false accuser, calumniator. The term reveals his malignant spirit which began in Eden. He slandered God to man when he questioned the goodness of God in forbidding them to eat the fruit of one tree. He also slanders man to God, and man to man, always attributing false motives.

4. **Satan**—meaning the "adversary" or the "opponent." The one who stands against, and works against, everything that is holy. He opposes all that is holy and right and true.

5. **Accuser**—of the brethren. He likes to accuse us to God. He accused both Joshua (Zechariah 3) and Job (Job 1) before God. He also likes to use us to accuse fellow believers. When we accuse others we line up with the Devil or the Accuser.

But God never leaves us defenceless. He gives us the secret of successfully and effectually dealing with this great adversary and clearly shows us three ways of dealing with him, overcoming him, and frustrating his diabolical working.

1. **Judicial weapon**—"Blood of the Lamb." This symbolizes a shameful, agonizing, violent death of the Son of God, the giving of His very life blood (violently poured out) when He became a sacrifice for sins upon the Cruel Cross and was buried but rose triumphantly over the grave and death that we might be free from the possession and oppression of the Devil. This is an all-powerful fact. We need to remember it and take it and use it to face our adversary.

2. **Evidential weapon**—"Word of Our Testimony." This suggests an open profession before others of something real in our life. Do you have a testimony? Today so many are shallow and there is no rejoicing in the resurrection power of the Cross. I have seen young people go to the mission field with nothing but the Bible and the word of their testimony and what transformation it wrought! It seems so weak, yet it is so powerful.

3. **Sacrificial weapon**—"Death to Self." Here we take the dagger and plunge it into our own lives. In John 12:24 Jesus said "Verily, verily, I say unto you, Except a corn of wheat fall into the ground and die, it abideth alone: but if it die, it bringeth forth much fruit." There needs to be a willingness, no matter if it costs us our lives, to carry the message of the Cross to regions beyond.

   Principle: "A church cold toward missions will soon find heathenism growing in its own ranks."

   John R. Mott said decades before World War II: "If we do not take the Bible to the Japanese we will have to take the sword." And that's what it was.

There were times in China when Clifford was called upon to cast out demons, which he did, but only in the power of prayer and the name of God, and by the word of God. As a young child, his eldest daughter, Elaine, remembered Clifford being called to the home of a demon-possessed woman. As the demon left, Elaine described the woman yelling and screaming, and clawing at her throat, then falling limp on the floor, foaming at the mouth and convulsing. Afterwards the woman was calm, spoke in her natural voice and resumed her normal activities. Sometimes demonic procession is difficult to distinguish from mental illness other than the person speaking in an abnormal voice, engaging in extreme self-injurious behaviour and displaying superhuman strength.

XVIII

War Experiences under Japanese Occupation

. . . The Lord is my helper, and I will not fear what man shall do unto me.

(HEBREWS 13:6)

In 1929 the Great Depression plunged Japan into an economic crisis. Its export markets were no longer available and it needed new markets for its goods, as well as raw materials for industrial development. With a searching eye, it cast its sights on China to meet both economic needs. China also fit well into Japan's political vision of an empire comprised entirely of Asian people and led by themselves.

In September 1931, Japan invaded Manchuria. Over the next two years, they added the northern provinces of Chahar, Jehol, and eastern Hopei to their holdings. But it was not until the summer of 1937 that a full-scale invasion of China took place, which became known as the Sino-Japanese War. It would last eight years, from 1937 to 1945.

In July 1937, Japanese forces attacked the cities of Peking and Tientsin in Hopei Province. From there they moved down the east coast of China taking all the port cities. Shanghai fell in November 1937, after three months of fierce fighting. Japanese forces then pushed west to Nanking, the capital of China. In retreat, the Chinese government moved nine hundred miles along the Yangtze River, to Chunking in Szechuan Province.

On December 13, 1937, the Japanese Army entered Nanking and a wholesale slaughter ensued. The occupation and decimation of Nanking has been referred to as "the rape of Nanking," with an estimated 300,000 Chinese civilians slaughtered in the most barbaric and savage manner. Women and small girls were raped repeatedly and then murdered. There were missionary casualties as well, one of whom was Minnie Vautrin.

Minnie was an educational missionary and taught at the Ginling Women's College in Nanking. When a Japanese attack of the city appeared inevitable, most of the foreigners left, but Minnie and a few others remained to help the Chinese people. They decided to set up an international safety zone around the college, which was deemed neutral and would provide safety for Chinese women and their families. When the city was attacked, thousands of refugees poured into the safety zone. Minnie and her small band of workers were responsible for securing food and fending off Japanese soldiers from attacking and raping them. Day and night she patrolled the grounds. Whenever she left the campus, she was accosted by Japanese authorities and soldiers, and exposed to the rapes and brutality that were occurring on the city's streets. The whole ordeal took an enormous toll on her—physically, mentally, and spiritually.

In May 1940 she suffered a nervous breakdown, which necessitated her return to the United States. While travelling across the Pacific Ocean, she repeatedly tried to kill herself by jumping over the side of the ship and had to be physically restrained. Back in the United States, she entered a psychiatric facility where she received electroshock therapy. When it was felt she was improving, she was released to her own care. On May 14, 1941, one year to the day she left Nanking, Minnie sealed the windows and doors of her home with tape, turned on the gas, and committed suicide.

The number of refugees fleeing the Japanese invasion was massive. Anyone along the coastal regions fled west, and then farther west as the Japanese armies moved inland. An estimated 25 to 40 million refugees, one of the largest migrations in history, fled for their lives. Dreyer writes about the

> . . . refugees, camping in the open fields with the rain pouring down, struggling to walk as far as possible each day as they fled inland. Many were old and decrepit. Here and there a filial son carrying his mother on his back. . . . Little children, tiny children, holding their parents' hands, munching moldy cabbage leaves. At intervals, prostrate along the side of the road, were those who were sick and dying. (p. 131)

Then there were the dead. Along with the mass migration came famine, which further ravaged the remaining population.

Japan's initial military objectives were to secure the port cities, which would landlock China, and take control of the major railway lines. Once in control of the railways, they would be able to move hundreds of thousands of troops, equipment, and supplies to various parts of the country. By 1939, all of this had been accomplished and the Japanese were able to push farther inland.

Clifford as a child.
Stewart, Gordon, Clifford,
Vernon and Hazel.
Circa 1911.

Clifford. Provost 1926

Florence and Clifford's
wedding picture, Calgary,
February 7, 1931

Florence, Philip and Clifford
just before leaving for China.
1934.

Elaine, Florence, Philip and Clifford, China.

Clifford preaching in China.

Philip, Clifford, Florence, Elaine and
baby Keith, Shanghai, 1939.

Florence, Clifford, Keith, Elaine and Philip
wearing his school uniform, Chefoo, 1940.

Elaine, Florence, Clifford, Blakely and Keith shortly
after their flight from China. 1944.

Back row: Florence, Blakely, Clifford
Front row: Keith, Bernard Paulson, Elaine, Gertrude Paulson

Back row: Elaine, Philip, Keith
Front row: Lucille, Clifford, Florence, Blakely,
upon Philip's return from China. 1946.

Back row: Florence,
Philip, Keith, Clifford
Middle row: Elaine,
Lucille, Blakely
Front row: Marguerite,
Duane. 1951.

Back row: Elaine, Keith, Philip
Front row: Clifford, Lucille, Duane, Marguerite, Blakely, Florence.
Saskatoon, circa 1956.

Clifford and Florence.
Saskatoon, circa 1950s.

Wuyi Mountains surrounding Shaowu which the
family had to cross when fleeing China.

Marguerite in China. 1987.

I HAVE SET WATCHMEN UPON THY WALLS, O JERUSALEM, WHICH SHALL NEVER HOLD THEIR PEACE DAY NOR NIGHT: YE THAT MAKE MEN- TION OF THE LORD, KEEP NOT SILENCE, AND GIVE HIM NO REST TILL HE ESTABLISH, AND TILL HE MAKE JERUSALEM A PRAISE IN THE EARTH. THE LORD HATH SWORN BY HIS RIGHT HAND, AND BY THE ARM OF HIS STRENGTH...

(*Is. 62; 6-8.*)

Sample of Clifford's penmanship.

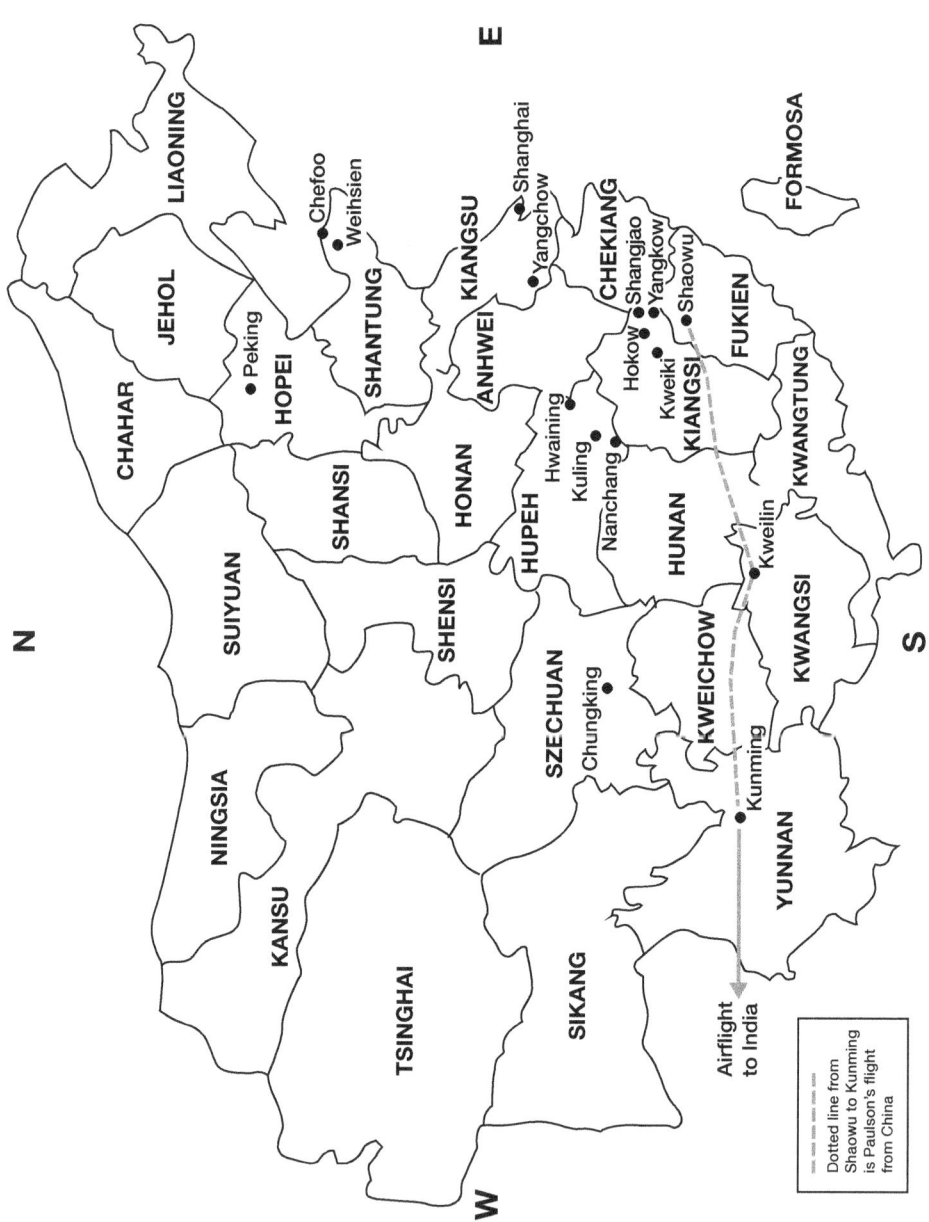

Map of China 1930

XIX

Son, Philip

And, behold, I am with thee, and will keep thee, in all the places whither thou goest . . .

(GENESIS 28:15)

In the summer of 1940, Clifford and Florence travelled overland from their home at Yangchow to Chefoo, a distance of 750 miles, to enroll Philip in the mission boarding school there. By this time a third child had been added to the family, Keith Beverly.

The city of Chefoo is situated in the northeast part of Shantung Province, on a protruding arm of land that points across the Yellow Sea toward Japan. It is a port city. Before the war, the harbour was filled with British and American ships, but now only Japanese vessels were anchored there.

Two hundred thousand people lived in Chefoo, a thousand of them foreigners. The city proper contained the Western business community— their business offices and residences. Their houses were white with red tile roofs and were spread out along the low-lying hills overlooking the bay. Next to them was a rather congested part of town containing the shabby homes of the Chinese. Off to the side, on a small secluded bay, was the mission school.

At that time, Chefoo and the province of Shantung were under Japanese control but it did not pose much of a problem for the school. Japan was at war with China, but not the rest of the world. The school operated normally and families travelled relatively freely between Free China (those parts of the country still under the control of the Chinese government) and Japanese-occupied China.

Philip was a rather shy and sensitive child. Because he had never been away from his parents before, they were glad to be able to stay with him for a while and help him adjust to his new surroundings. But the time came too soon for their goodbye. Although reassured that he would be happy and well cared for, parting from their first born was difficult. Another CIM missionary, Isobel Kuhn, in taking her own young child to Chefoo, stated, "Had it not been for the Great Comforter that fills the ache in the heart of the child and the parents, it would have been unbearable. Although the mind says, a child needs education, the heart says, but he is too young." Besides, the parents have their work to do, and God is the far better parent anyway. The one saving grace was that Philip and most of the other children at Chefoo would return home for holiday seasons and summer vacations whenever possible and if the distance was not too great.

Philip's time at school was spent making friends, playing, doing his school work, and engaging in various sports, as well as writing letters home to his parents. In addition to his regular academic subjects, Philip took Latin, French, art, music, and scripture.

Clifford and Florence did not see Philip that year for Christmas, as it had only been a few months since they dropped him off. For those children who had to remain at school over the holidays, the school put on a festive Christmas celebration, complete with carollers, a Christmas tree, a goose dinner, plum pudding, and of course, Santa Claus.

In December of 1941, when Japan attacked Pearl Harbor, declaring war on the United States, Chefoo School was no longer considered neutral. It became the property of the Imperial Japanese Army. Soldiers marched in and took charge of it while guards, holding rifles and extending bayonets, were posted at the front entrance. The headmaster, Patrick Bruce, was ordered to turn over the senior girls to serve as prostitutes[71] for the Japanese military. He refused. Fortunately there were no repercussions for his actions.

Because of the war, the school was unable to obtain further funding from mission headquarters, and food for the children had to be rationed. Eventually,

---

[71] The Japanese government and military operated brothels for their service men in occupied territories. Typically, the women were procured from the captured populations. Had Mr. Bruce not adamantly refused to turn over the older female students or, if they had been taken anyway by force, they would have been used for sexual purposes. The official term for these women was "comfort women," whereas the service men generally referred to them as "public toilets." Brothels were considered an important component of warfare, in that they served to reduce incidences of rape and subsequent international criticism, contain venereal disease—which was rampant among the troops—and reward soldiers fighting on the battlefields.

what funds the school had on hand were depleted. Staff and students turned to God, meeting for a special evening of prayer to ask for guidance and provision. Later that evening, some Chinese Christians, at great peril to themselves, threw several sacks of peanuts over the wall. Inside one of the sacks was six hundred dollars in Chinese currency. Although the school was under Japanese rule, it was definitely in God's hands.

For some time the Japanese Army had been using poisonous gas to subdue the population in Shantung Province and other areas of northeast China. Even more sinister, they were doing experimental research with human subjects[72] obtained from local populations. This included prisoners of war, infants, and children. It is entirely likely that the students from Chefoo would have been used for these experiments had they not been considered a viable commodity for prisoner exchanges.

On November 1, 1942, Japanese authorities ordered the closure of the school, giving staff five days to make all necessary preparations. The children packed their belongings, then on November 5, walked under Japanese military escort to their new home, a former American Presbyterian mission compound at Temple Hill. It was to be a holding area for the students and staff. The children walked in pairs, each carrying their own bedroll, uncertain of what was really happening. They walked along the beach and through town. Crowds of Chinese lined the streets to stare at the little white children who marched as if on their way to church but now as prisoners of Japanese soldiers. The townspeople were used to being harassed and mistreated by the soldiers, but they had never seen foreign children and adults treated in the same manner. Especially unusual was the sound of the children singing as they marched along.

> God is still on the throne, and He will remember his own.
> Though trials may press us and burdens distress us, He never will leave us alone.
> God is still on the throne, and He will remember His own.
> His promise is true, He will not forget you, God is still on the throne.[73]

Their new home was a large compound containing several houses and other buildings. It was surrounded by a stone wall topped with barbed wire and guarded by armed soldiers. Once settled, the children began a routine that

---

[72] Appendix E.
[73] Hymn, words, and music written by Mrs. F.W. Suffield.

included chores and school lessons, which the teachers diligently continued to pursue with them. But life was not the same. The food was basic—typically bean curd, coarse millet bread, and cabbage—and the children became malnourished and sickly. The premises were cold, the rooms crowded, and sanitation was lacking. The children's clothes quickly disintegrated into rags.

Despite the hardships they faced, the children were still able to have some fun at the expense of their captors. One of Philip's classmates recounted their mischievousness at roll call, when they were required to number themselves in Japanese:

> ... those of us at the younger end of the school always ran out at the roll-call signal, to get to the front of the line. When the commandant in all his military braid and finery and with his attendant officers marched up, one of the soldiers with appropriate air-sucking preliminaries shouted out, "Bango" which meant "Number off!" Away we went, as fast as we could go: "Ichi, nee, san, she, go, roku, etc." The first four in the line-up could play a joke with the numbers. Instead of counting "Ichi, nee, san, she," we would sometimes say, "Itchy knee, scratch a flea."[74]

Ten months later, on September 7, 1943, the students and staff were relocated to a larger compound near Weihsien, farther south and about one hundred miles inland. The trip took them three days travelling by boat, train, and army truck. During this time, Clifford, Florence, and their remaining children were attempting a trek across China, fleeing from the encroaching Japanese Army.

Similar to Temple Hill, Weihsien compound was a former American Presbyterian mission. It was surrounded by a six-foot-high brick wall, with newly erected guard towers and small rectangular openings cut in the walls for machine guns to fire through. Search lights were mounted on the towers and coiled electrified barbed wire ran along the top of the wall, outside of which was a large trench. Later, more electrified barbed wire would be added to the other side of the trench.

Once again, Philip's life was confined by walls and armed guards, and controlled by orders. There were harsh rules and long queues for most everything. He had to line up for meals, to have his eating utensils washed, to use the outdoor toilets, and for roll call. There were still chores to do

---

[74] Michel, p. 54.

and school lessons to participate in, which the teachers taught solely from memory.

The food was lacking in nutrition and quantity, and was barely sufficient to sustain life. There was dried bread, tea (that was closer to water), and soups and stews made from meat that was usually half-spoiled and maggot-ridden, and included skin, fat, and the innards. Usually the meat was horse or mule; even fish bones were fried for food. Then there were the vegetables—gnarled potatoes, bitter-tasting greens, and rotting eggplant or cabbage. Weeds were collected from the compound and used as a vegetable. Because the diet was lacking in calcium, the shells from black market eggs were collected and ground into powder to feed to the children. One time Philip traded his only pair of shoes for an egg and actually got to eat all of it and not just the shell.

The children and other internees ate in one of several large dining rooms. Each person had to supply their own cup, bowl or plate, and cutlery. Often tin cans or even soap dishes served as mugs or bowls. The line for meals was always long, sometimes stretching as far as seventy yards with a wait time of three quarters of an hour. The dining halls constantly smelled of sewage, which wafted in from the open cesspools outside.

Adequate clothing was also a concern as clothes wore out or were outgrown quickly. New clothes had to be made from whatever material was at hand. Thus, old curtains and mattress covers became new shirts, blankets became trousers, and tablecloths, underwear.

Other than the primitive living conditions, three incidents marred Philip's life in camp. The first happened when Philip entered a restricted area to retrieve a ball. A prison guard, seeing him, twisted his arm at the elbow leaving it permanently injured. The second was the death of one of the older students. On August 16, 1944, sixteen-year-old Brian Thompson was awaiting roll call when he playfully grabbed an electric wire hanging overhead. Although the circuit was only 110 volts, the ground was wet and Brian was shoeless. He was electrocuted. Philip quickly learned that death comes to the young as well and not only the very old. Then on February 21, 1945, Eric Lidell,[75] Philip's math and science teacher at Weihsien, died from a brain tumor.

---

[75] Eric Liddell was the famous gold medalist of the 400-metre sprint in the 1924 Paris Olympics who refused to run on Sunday, and hero of the movie *Chariots of Fire*.

XX

Flight from Japanese Attack

Thou shalt not be afraid for the terror by night; nor for the arrow that flieth by day . . .

(PSALM 91:5)

In the latter part of 1940, the Paulsons moved to Shangjao, also known as Shangrao. Like Kweiki and Hokow, it was situated on the Kwangsin River and was a communication hub for railway and boat travel. Although it had a small population of some 10,000 people, it had increased in size when large numbers of refugees arrived seeking safety from war-torn eastern China. Within one hundred miles of the town were hundreds of smaller towns and villages, all of them without the gospel.

The mission station was in the old part of town, where houses were crowded close together along narrow, winding streets. The town was surrounded by a high, wide wall patrolled by sentries and encircled by a small moat. Several gates led in and out of town, to the newer sections.

The Shangjao mission station was a large, walled compound with rooms along the inside walls and a garden area at its centre. A large wooden gate led into the compound, which was left open during the day for visitors and meetings. Inside the front gate was a great hall where people would come to inquire about the gospel, buy Bibles, or seek food and safety. The compound contained quarters for the family and servants, guest rooms for travelling missionaries, a chapel, a school, and a study room for Clifford to prepare his sermons, study the Bible, and personally meet with people. Refugees were frequent visitors.

In the early 1940s, Japanese forces, having secured control of northeast China and all major ports along the coast, started to move farther inland, heading west along the Yangtze River and into the southern part of the country. With the intent of capturing Kiangsi, they started a bombing campaign in the northern part of the province. The procedure of attack was predictable. First, planes might fly over and drop pamphlets asking for surrender and promising that no harm would come to the people. Of course, if they surrendered, they quickly learned otherwise. Next, military planes would come with their blitzkrieg bombing and strafing, the intent being to cow the populace. Afterwards, the army would march in and take over the area with little resistance.

When Japanese planes were heard in the distance, a large bell would be rung, warning of impending attack. Town criers with their shrill voices would yell, "Fei-chi lai-la! Fei-chi lai-la," at which hundreds of citizens would rush out of their homes and crowd the narrow streets, seeking refuge outside the city walls. There, in the surrounding hills and countryside, they would hide in holes dug into the hillsides.

In Shangjao the bombings were constant. Sometimes they were daily and would go on for several weeks with upwards of forty-five planes at a time. The bombs in themselves were deadly, killing people outright, decimating houses, and leaving large holes in the ground. But the shrapnel from explosions was worse—it would lodge in the body, resulting in a huge loss of blood, extreme pain, and a slow, excruciating death.

In an article written for the CIM periodical *China's Millions*,[76] Florence wrote of one specific raid, which destroyed their home and necessitated a move to Yangkow.

> About that time we heard air raid warnings almost daily, as our city was the headquarters for the Third Military War Zone, but one Friday in April, 1941, the rapid clanging of the urgent alarm warned us of imminent danger. I hurried out of our house with a Chinese boy who was wheeling our youngest child in a bamboo wheelbarrow; while my husband locked up the house, put our little girl on the handle bars of his bicycle, and started off for the north gate of the city. In the crush of fleeing humanity we became separated. When we were about 150 yards from the gate, the soldiers cried out for all to hide as the roaring of enemy planes could be heard. The Chinese boy ran for the path into the

---

[76] December, 1944, p. 182.

garden below, taking our baby with him, but when he saw me pushing on in face of the soldiers, who are ordered to shoot anyone who moves while the planes are overhead, he followed after me. One desperate effort and we were all out of the gate, but still had a ravine to cross and a grave-covered hillside to scale before reaching the dugouts, which looked like rabbit holes. We had no sooner ducked our heads under the small clay roofs, some of us crouching in muddy water, than the roar of planes overhead was heard. We could see the twenty-seven planes in relays of nine circle round and round, then heard the whine of falling bombs and the zoom! of their explosions. The bombing continued about forty minutes, but it seemed like hours. Before going back to the city we climbed the hill to judge, by the ascending smoke, where the bombs had struck. The coolie's son, who attended the children's service, came to me crying: "Our house is hit! Our house is destroyed and I can't find my mother or my baby brother or sister!" We comforted him as best we could but found out later it was not his home but our compound that had been hit. A bomb had fallen just where the Chinese boy and our baby had left the path and sought refuge in the garden. How we thank God that we were able to get out of the city!

We arrived home to find our compound a mass of ruins. The first thing we did was to search for two old Christians who, too feeble to flee, had hid under the bedding. The room next to them was demolished and the tiles of their room had fallen on the bed. They were badly shaken but neither had received a scratch. A goose sitting on eggs in the same room was still in the same position.

The front of our house, the school and teachers' dwellings were gone, and the church and chapel roofs damaged. Back of the school, the evangelists kept pigs: the roof of the sty had fallen and crushed a few of them, but in order that nothing be wasted a man was already preparing one to be eaten. An incendiary bomb had fallen just outside the window of my husband's study and we could not go into the house because it had not exploded. We called the police but as they could not come immediately we stood out among the ruins. We had eaten nothing since early morning and it was seven o'clock in the evening before we could sit down to a meal. The incendiary was fused out the next day.

Although Clifford and Florence never detailed the horrors they experienced—the carnage, the sights and sounds of the dead and dying—other missionaries have. One such missionary was Duncan McRoberts. In his two books, *While China Bleeds* and *Pleading China*, he wrote:

> Bombs had fallen and the dead and dying lay tangled around the small craters.

> Bombs would leave huge holes in the ground while, with the explosion, shrapnel would lodge into the bodies.

> The wounded groaned and moaned; the desperate cursed or wept, while an occasional eerie scream filled the air.

Shangjao fell the end of May 1942. The fighting was said to have been fierce and resulted in a mass exodus of the local population.

After a year of constant bombing and the noise of cannon fire, along with the loss of their home, the family moved thirty-five li[77] to Yangkow; however, their safety was short-lived. Several months after their arrival, the Japanese military moved into northern Kiangsi, and Yangkow was directly in their line of fire. Again bombs started to fall and the roads surged with refugees. Florence and Clifford hastily packed their clothes, bedding, and a few utensils and fled to the nearby Kwangsin River. Haste was essential, for even as they were leaving, the Chinese military set up a large field gun in front of their house in a vain attempt to slow the Japanese advance. At the river, the family boarded a small boat to Hokow. The invading Japanese forces followed, bombing them and strafing with their machine guns, attempting to sink the boats on the river. Their intent—complete havoc, destruction, and the annihilation of anyone in their path.

Margaret Crossett, in her book *Harvest at the Front*, described a similar scene relayed to her by several female refugees:

> The planes would fly over and circle the city low and then move slowly across the city following the main street from the south to the north, dropping bombs every few feet. Many people were killed as the streets were crowded. Some ran to the river and got on boats but the planes bombed the boats and sank them, and many more were drowned. Some fled into the willow groves and tried to hide, but the planes bombed the groves and many more were killed and wounded. Some just ran along

---

[77] A li is one-third of a mile.

the road but the planes followed and bombed them and they were killed too. (pp. 31–32, paraphrased)

It was well known among the Chinese population and missionaries alike that in whatever area was occupied by the Japanese Army, there would be wanton looting, the murder of innocent civilians, destruction of property, and rape. Which was why, when it was announced the Japanese were coming, whole villages, towns, and cities would flee. Some people would even commit suicide. Usually those left behind were either too old or weak to flee or they intended to loot the homes of those who'd fled. Masses of people crowded the roadways or fled by small boats on the river.

Miraculously, the Paulsons escaped any injury and arrived safely in Hokow. There, they met up with three other missionaries, but because they were still close to the front lines—they could hear the sound of Japanese field guns nearby—they decided to make their way overland to a small outstation another seventy li away. By this time, Blake had been born but was still under a year old. Keith was three, Elaine six. Travel was difficult with the little ones. Fortunately, they were able to obtain seven wheelbarrows to help carry their belongings and the children. It was the time of year when the river seasonally flooded, as such the fields were ankle deep in water; pushing the wheelbarrows was exhausting. They had no food and could only buy rice gruel at exorbitant prices. Pangs of hunger were ever present.

Reaching the outstation, they decided to stay on for several weeks to recuperate. Later, they were joined by six additional female missionaries—they now numbered eleven adults and three small children. Again there was little food to purchase and no means of obtaining money, so they decided to move on to somewhere with telegraphic and postal communications. They remained in front of the Japanese forces, albeit just; haste was imperative. Every ounce of energy was used in an attempt to gain greater distance. The adults walked but were fortunate enough to hire coolies to ferry the young children in two baskets. Keith remembers the baskets being uncomfortable—with each step of the coolie they were jostled from one side of the basket to the other. Because the coolies were afraid to travel far, Clifford had to travel back with them to their place of origin, then travel back to Florence and the others, hire another set of coolies to carry the children a few more miles, and then repeat the whole process over and over again. They walked for nine days.

Jap planes followed us, machine gunning us as we went. . . . We were forced to hide behind shrubs, and in ditches by the road side. We lived on rice and green vegetables because the countryside was stripped by retreating Chinese armies.[78]

The Chinese soldiers themselves posed a threat to the travelling missionaries. Underpaid and underfed, the soldiers pillaged and robbed the fleeing refugees—they were no different from the bandits that roamed the area.

Added to their own misery and plight were the scenes of horror they encountered along the way.

One could hear the despairing cries of the doomed distinctly above the rattle of the gunfire.

The dead lay where they died, those minimally wounded would stumble along while the fatally wounded moaned and groaned as blood oozed from their wounds.

I will never forget heart-broken mothers as they staggered along clinging the bloody bundles of cloth, bone and flesh, all that was left of their precious children.[79]

Upon arriving at their specified destination, Clifford was unable to find suitable premises to rent, so the family left Kiangsi Province and moved to the city of Shaowu, in Fukien Province. There they worked with the American Board Mission for six months doing evangelical work. As long as the war continued, Elaine was not able to attend school; Florence taught her at home. Both parents were recovering from malaria while Keith was recovering from malaria and dysentery. In a brief letter to her mother, Florence wrote "God is ever faithful and nothing can happen to us except He allows it."

---

[78] Interview given by Clifford after the family's return to Canada in *The Lethbridge Herald,* Rev. Clifford T. Paulson, Back in Alberta, Tells of Escape from Japs, April 1, 1944, p. 9.

[79] McRoberts.

XXI

Burial of the Doolittle Raiders

*He shall cover thee with his feathers, and under his wings shalt
thou trust . . .*

(PSALM 91:4)

On April 18, 1942, the United States of America launched a surprise bombing
attack on the home islands of Japan. It was four months after Pearl Harbor,
which marked the United States' official entry into WWII. The attack
involved sixteen B-25 Mitchell bombers, which took off from a Navy aircraft
carrier situated in Japanese waters. The planes would fly first over Japan,
bombing various military and industrial targets, before moving on to China
for refuelling. Several makeshift landing strips were to be prepared near the
coast of China, in Chekiang Province, and homing beacons were to be used
to guide the pilots in.

Each bomber had a five-man crew, including a pilot, co-pilot, navigator,
bombardier, and gunner, all under the leadership of Lieutenant Colonel James
"Jimmy" Doolittle. The mission was called the "Doolittle Raid," the men
"Doolittle Raiders."

At 0820 hours on the morning of April 18, the bombers left the carrier at
five-minute intervals. After bombing their respective targets, they proceeded
southwest along the southern coast of Japan and across the East China Sea
toward eastern China and the makeshift airstrips supposedly awaiting them.

Of the sixteen aircraft, twelve finally reached the Chinese coast but were
unable to find the airstrips. The night was dark with thick fog and rain,
and the terrain was unfamiliar. The men had been in the air approximately
fourteen hours and flown nonstop a distance of 2,200 miles. Unbeknownst
to them, the Chinese were not prepared for their landing and the airstrips

were unmanned. There were no lights, beacons, or landing flares—only total darkness. Although Chiang Kai-shek had been informed that the United States needed several airfields on the Chinese coast for the landing of American planes, for purposes of secrecy, he had not been informed of the actual raid on Japan or when the fields were to be ready.

All twelve planes that made it to land crashed in the mountains when they ran out of fuel. Another three planes crashed in the ocean not far from shore, while one other flew to Russia as it was closer and the plane was already dangerously low on fuel.

Each crew was named for the order in which its plane left the carrier. Dooittle left first and was crew number one. After dropping his bombs on a factory in Japan, he flew west, reaching the coast of China after dark. By 2130 hours, fuel was low and he was unable to find the airfields in the heavy fog, so he ordered his crew to bail out and crashed his B-25 into a nearby mountainside. He was seventy miles north of Chuchow, near Tein Mu Shen. He jumped from 6,200 feet and landed in a rice paddy that had been freshly fertilized with human excrement and recently ploughed. He remained close by for the night. At dawn the next day, he followed a well-worn path to a small village. Coming upon a Chinese man who could not speak any English, he drew a picture of a train on a piece of paper. The man smiled and nodded, and then led him to a small Chinese military detachment where help was provided to locate the rest of his crew.

After learning that some of the men from the other crews had been captured, Doolittle offered a reward of $2,000 in Chinese currency and tried to persuade a local commander to send troops to rescue them. All efforts were futile. Doolittle and his crew then set out for Chuchow. They found a riverboat and hid in its cabin until free of Japanese-held territory. While docking near a small village, a Caucasian man in Chinese garb entered the boat, having been alerted by a local citizen that there were Americans on board. The young man was John Birch,[80] an American missionary residing in the nearby city of Shangjao. Birch agreed to accompany Doolittle and his men part of the way to Chuchow and to act as their interpreter and liaison with the Chinese Army. He was also able to arrange a military escort for them the rest of the way to Chungking.

---

[80] Appendix F.

On his way to Chuchow, Doolittle located and met with Clifford. Doolittle gave him the $2,000 intended as the reward for the captured American airmen. With that enterprise proving fruitless, Doolittle decided to use the money for the burial costs of his dead airmen. He instructed Clifford to give the money to Birch to buy a plot of land and arrange the burials. By then Birch had returned to Shangjao, where he received a telegram from the American Military Mission in Chungking ordering him to report to the nearest air base at Chuchow. While there, he found two more crews of Doolittle's men and was assisting them in a flight to Chungking when "a phone call came from a Canadian missionary friend, Reverend C. T. Paulson, at the town of Yangkow. 'Doolittle was just here on his way to Chungking and left some money and special instructions for you,' Paulson informed him. 'How soon can you come?'" On April 30, "the next day the Canadian missionary handed him the $2,000 in Chinese money left by Colonel Doolittle with his orders: 'You are to bury Corporal Leland D. Faktor[81] and any others who may be brought in for burial, arrange medical aid for any injured, obtain all information possible on missing aviators, serve as secretary/translator to aviators stopping over at Ch'u Hsien,[82] accompany the last crew to Chungking, and report to the Military Mission there'".[83]

Of the sixteen crews, two met with the cruelest of fates. Crew number six, piloted by Dean Hallmark, left the Naval carrier at 0845 hours and by 1230 hours was dropping its bombs on a steel mill in Tokyo. Although the crew would have preferred to attack the Japanese Imperial Palace, they had strict orders from Doolittle that it was not to be bombed. Other members of the crew included Robert Meder, the co-pilot; Chase Nielsen, navigator; Donald Fitzmaurice, engineer gunner; and William Dieter, bombardier.

Leaving Japan, crew six flew toward China, but when their fuel ran out, they crash landed four miles off shore, along the coast of Japanese-occupied China. It was a fast, hard landing. Hallmark, still in his seat, was catapulted through the windshield and into the water, but he was able to extract himself and, along with Meder and Nielsen, climb on top of the submerging plane. Dieter, the bombardier, had been in the plexiglass nose section, which

---

[81] Corporal Leland Faktor was the gunner on crew number three. He died when bailing out of his plane and was later buried by John Birch.

[82] Also known as Chuchow.

[83] Hefley, pp. 89–90.

sustained the most damage. He was thrown into the water. Although seriously injured and incoherent, he was able to climb up on the cowling of the right engine. Fitzmaurice exited the plane by the rear side window. He had a large gash on his forehead; Nielsen helped him on top of the right wing. The water was choppy with twelve- to fifteen-foot waves that soon washed the men into the sea. Dieter was able to swim part of the way to shore but succumbed to his injuries and drowned. His body was washed ashore by the tide. Meder was able to grab Fitzmaurice by his life jacket and swim to shore with him, only to discover that he had already died.

The three surviving crew members—Hallmark, Meder, and Nielsen—made it to shore but were quickly apprehended by armed Chinese guerillas. Although the guerillas operated in Japanese-controlled China, they were not necessarily loyal to the Japanese authorities, nor, for that matter, to the Chinese government; they were loyal only to themselves and their own mercenary interests. Because the captured airmen were worth a significant reward and goodwill, they were turned over to the Japanese Army. Crew number sixteen, piloted by William Farrow, was also captured by the Japanese.[84]

After crew number six crashed in the ocean, the bodies of Fitzmaurice and Dieter, who had been left on the beach, were removed by the Chinese. Two wooden boxes were prepared as coffins for them. The Chinese Christians approached Clifford and asked that he perform a Christian burial service for the two Americans. To protect themselves and their families from Japanese reprisal, as well as fearing that the Japanese would find the bodies and desecrate them, they kept the burial a secret. The Chinese Christians led Clifford from his home in the middle of the night through the mountainous terrain. He was blindfolded for his own protection, to keep him from knowing the exact burial site. The Chinese men carried the coffins. The path was narrow and treacherous as the men trudged upwards in silence. Clifford was apprehensive. He knew the potential costs: if they were discovered it would mean a torturous death for all, including the villagers and their families below. But he was propelled by his faith in God and prepared for whatever might happen. The small procession stopped at a discrete clearing. The graves, which had been dug earlier in the day, were ready to receive the men. The Chinese Christians removed Clifford's blindfold, and there,

---

[84] Appendix G.

on the mountainside, they buried Fitzmaurice and Dieter. Clifford did not know the names of the dead men or anything about them, only that they were downed airmen from an American plane that had crashed in the East China Sea. Clifford said a short prayer for the young men and their families, and quoted several verses of scripture. Possibly he even quoted a favourite poem of his, which he had also copied in calligraphy and sent home to his mother in Canada, upon the death of his younger brother, Stewart: "Crossing the Bar," by Alfred, Lord Tennyson.

Crossing the Bar

Sunset and evening star,
And one clear call for me!
And may there be no moaning of the bar,
When I put out to sea,

But such a tide as moving seems asleep,
Too full for sound and foam,
When that which drew from out the boundless deep
Turns again home.

Twilight and evening bell,
And after that the dark!
And may there be no sadness of farewell,
When I embark;

For though from out our bourne of Time and Place
The flood may bear me far,
I hope to see my Pilot face to face
When I have crossed the bar.

Clifford did not speak of the burial until long after the war, the secrecy of the mission having been emphasized by Lieutenant Colonel Doolittle. Nor did the American government release the full details of the raid for a year afterwards, out of concern for Japanese reprisal against both the Chinese people and the missionaries who had assisted the men. Clifford had no doubts about the fate that awaited him and his family, especially Philip, already interned in a prison camp, if Japanese officials discovered his role in the burial of Dieter and Fitzmaurice, and his contact with Doolittle.

True to form, the Japanese began a campaign of terror in the areas where the Doolittle Raiders had landed and travelled. It became known as the Zhejiang-Jiangxi campaign and lasted from mid-May to early September 1942. It was a campaign of death and destruction in retaliation for the bombing of Japan and Chinese complicity in it. Its purpose was threefold: to punish anyone who had assisted the Raiders; to set an example for the Chinese people, should there be further such incidents; and to prevent future operations using Chinese airfields by systematically destroying them.

Moving inland some 200 miles, the Japanese Army painstakingly covered the territory where the Raiders had landed. Fifty-three Japanese battalions traversed twenty thousand square miles across the provinces of Chekiang and Kiangsi. By the time they left three months later, 250,000 Chinese peasants were dead and the entire countryside had been decimated.

The Chinese people who had assisted the American airmen were easily identified by the gifts they'd received: cigarettes, coins, and candy, which the men had given them in appreciation—all telltale signs of the Americans' presence. Details abound of the atrocities committed.

> At Ihwang[85] in Kiangsi Province, the Japanese found the man who had given shelter to Lieutenant Harold F. Watson. They wrapped him in blankets, poured kerosene on him and forced his wife to set him afire. At this village they also threw hundreds of people into deep wells, destroyed American mission property in the vicinity, and desecrated the graves in a missionary cemetery.[86]

Father Wendelin Dunker, a local priest, observed the atrocities first-hand:

> They shot any man, woman, child, cow, hog, or just about anything that moved. They raped any woman from the ages of 10–65. . . . None of the humans shot were buried either, but were left to lay on the ground to rot, along with the hogs and cows.[87]

In Nancheng, a city of fifty thousand, soldiers forced a group of Chinese men who had provided food for the airmen to eat fecal matter before lining them up for a "bullet contest"—to see how many people a single bullet could

---

[85] Ihwang is situated between Kweiki and Hokow in the heart of the Paulsons' missionary work.
[86] Hefley, p. 90.
[87] Scott, p. 381.

pass through before it stopped. The Japanese troops occupied Nancheng for one month, raping, killing, and looting. Afterwards they razed the city to the ground. The city of Ying Tan was also destroyed simply because the Catholic mission there, operated by Father William J. Glynn, had assisted crew number thirteen. In Chuchow,[88] which was Doolittle's intended destination, the Japanese air force conducted 1,131 raids, killing thousands of civilians and destroying large sections of the city.

Anyone who had helped the Americans was marked for death, and any village where the airmen had rested or simply passed through was to be destroyed. Out of twenty-eight market towns in the area, twenty-five were destroyed completely. Thousands of oxen and pigs were slaughtered, crops burned, vital irrigation systems wrecked, and bridges, roads and railway lines torn up. All the airfields in the area were dug up, with the Japanese forcing 4,000 coolies to dig wide trenches at right angles to the runways. The devastation was so severe that it was easier to build new runways than it was to repair existing ones.

Even after Japanese forces left the area, the destruction did not end. As the ground troops withdrew to other parts of the province, the bacteriological warfare units commenced their work. Anthrax, plague, cholera and typhoid pathogens were used to infect wells and rivers, and contaminated food was laid out as though left behind by the troops for the starving peasants to eat.

Chiang Kai-shek "was furious at the havoc and slaughter of his people. In a cable to the United States Government he wrote: 'After they had been caught unawares by the falling of bombs on Tokyo, Japanese troops attacked the coastal regions of China where many of the American flyers had landed. These Japanese troops slaughtered every man, woman and child in those areas—let me repeat—these Japanese troops slaughtered every man, woman and child in those areas.'"[89] In all, hundreds of thousands of Chinese civilians were massacred by the Japanese Army in their search for the downed bomber crews and in retaliation for any assistance provided to them.

---

[88] Chuchow eventually fell to the Japanese military in May 1942.
[89] Glines (1964), p. 318.

XXII

Flight from China

Be strong and of a good courage; be not afraid, neither be thou dismayed: for the Lord thy God is with thee whithersoever thou goest.

(JOSHUA 1:9)

For the time being the family was relatively safe in Shaowu, but Clifford was under no delusions regarding his family's fate if the Japanese were to learn of his assistance to the Doolittle Raiders. If they were captured and it was ascertained that he was the "white man" the soldiers were actively looking for, they would all be imprisoned or executed—even Philip in Weihsien. Besides, they had been in China more than nine years and their furlough was long overdue—seven years was the usual term of service, after which each missionary was expected to return to his home country for a year.

It was the end of summer 1943. Japan was in control of eastern China and all the port cities, as well as the Burma Road. The only way out of China was to cross the width of the country to Kunming in the west and then fly over the Himalayan Mountains to India. Had the family delayed their journey for any length of time they would have been trapped in the east, as Japan was rapidly moving into the central and southern parts of China; if successful, Japan's expansion would cut off the Paulsons' only exit route.

The young family's travel would prove to be lengthy and perilous, a good portion of it on foot. The distance from Shaowu to Kunming was over a thousand miles. In Kunming they would have to try to access a flight to India, either on an army or cargo plane. The number of army planes was limited, but there were numerous cargo flights. Before the Burma Road was lost to the Japanese, over twenty thousand tons of supplies were trucked monthly into China. Afterwards, cargo planes had to transport everything and could only take small loads, which meant more planes and more chances to catch a flight out of the country.

Between Shaowu and Kunming, much of the travel was difficult—the terrain around Shaowu was mountainous. Farther on, there were more mountains to cross, rivers to ford, and rugged countryside to traverse, all the while the war with Japan still raging around them. Matters were made worse by the ages of the children—Elaine was seven, Keith four, and Blake one-and-a-half. Florence was also pregnant with her fifth child, and the entire family suffered periodic bouts of malaria.

As it came time to leave, Florence packed their things in several carrying cases and left them on the second-floor veranda overnight, in preparation to leave early in the morning. During the night, thieves stole what few belongings they had, leaving the family with only the clothes on their backs and a few remaining items that could be carried by hand. Fortunately, they still had their medicine kit and a bit of food with which to start their journey. It also helped that all of them spoke fluent Chinese, which made it easier to seek direction and obtain assistance when needed.

The mountains of northern Kiangsi posed a real hardship for the family, and each day's progress was laborious and limited. The narrow, well-worn dirt paths, which led from village to village, wound up and down and around the mountains. Small groups of Japanese soldiers were still in the vicinity, and Clifford never knew when rounding a bend in the road if he would come face to face with a Japanese patrol. All he knew was that he had to push on to the west, toward Kweilin. It was the first major city on their route out of China, a distance of some six hundred miles.

For the first part of their journey, Clifford pedalled Elaine and Keith on an old bicycle, while Florence walked carrying Blake. At other times they all walked, although one of the parents still had to carry Blake because of his age. At some twenty pounds, he seemed much heavier with each mile, yet the family trudged on. They walked and cycled and walked some more, only stopping for brief periods to rest and care for the children. Sores developed on their feet and their muscles ached. Slowly the tires of the bicycle wore out and it had to be abandoned.

Most of the small villages along the way were deserted or had been destroyed by the Japanese Army in their search for the Doolittle Raiders. Little remained of the once-active communities, and the devastated countryside left no place to obtain lodging or food. If there were any inns, they were already filled with refugees, and if there was any food to be had, it was costly and of poor quality. Although Clifford had a few coins and some paper bills on hand, one of which was printed at a million yen, inflation[90] meant it was of little value—worth only about one American dollar.

Food and water were their most pressing needs and often the most difficult to obtain. All family members had to keep up their strength—the parents so they could keep going, and the children so they could manage as much as possible on their own. If food was available and they had money, the family would buy a small amount, often just a little bowl of rice to share. Vegetables, usually half-rotten, were scavenged from fields along the way. The vegetables had to be wiped as clean as possible because of the human waste used to fertilize the crops. Risk of contamination was high and dysentery[91] a real possibility.

Thirst was ever present. Since sewage was regularly dumped into the streams and rivers, the water was undrinkable on its own. The family had nothing with which to boil water, so hot water or tea had to be bought. Despite contamination, the streams along the way allowed them to bathe occasionally and wash their clothes, even though the same clothes had to be put on afterwards. Over time, their clothes became thin and worn and were insufficient for colder weather. When it rained, they became soaked through, and when the sun burned down on them, they were at risk of heatstroke.[92] Clifford already had suffered heatstroke once and remembered the mental confusion and headaches it caused, let alone the close call with death.

Accommodations for sleep were usually a ditch, a field beside the road, an abandoned or burnt-out house, or a clump of trees. Elaine remembers frequently sleeping under bridges. For warmth, the children slept between their parents. Any belongings had to be safely tucked away, otherwise they

---

90 As the war dragged on with Japan, inflation soared. The Chinese government was printing money indiscriminately, and Chinese banks were undervaluing foreign funds. Before the war, four dollars of Chinese National Currency (CNC) was equivalent to one dollar US funds. This valuation decreased dramatically; by 1942/43 one million Chinese dollars equated to one US dollar, and by 1948 three million CNC to the American dollar.

91 Dysentery is a serious medical condition caused by inflammation of the intestines. Symptoms include pain, diarrhea and bloody stools, fever and dehydration. If untreated, it can be fatal.

92 Heatstroke is caused by overexertion or prolonged periods of time spent under a hot sun. In such conditions the body overheats and produces symptoms of dizziness, headaches and excessive perspiration. In extreme cases it can result in mental confusion, coma, seizures and death.

would be stolen by Chinese peasants or refugees. Along the way, the family's medicine kit and various sundry items were taken.

After getting what little sleep they could, the family would arise in the morning chilled and shivering, with soiled, damp clothing and aching, stiff limbs. Once they were fortunate to find refuge at a Catholic mission, but they had to sleep on coffins already occupied by the dead.

As each day passed, the members of the family weakened. Malnutrition and exhaustion were particularly hard on Florence and the development of her unborn baby. She was also suffering from morning sickness. Having crossed through Kiangsi Province, the family travelled into southern Hunan. The route taken was never direct but rather circuitous, as they had to skirt around areas known to have a Japanese presence. Of course, the countryside was different, but not the devastation from Japanese aerial attack. It was always the same and would be the same along the entire route the family travelled.

Stretches of road were filled with refugees, all fleeing the Japanese onslaught. Upon hearing the familiar drone of the planes, people would scramble from the roadway and seek refuge wherever they could. The bombing came quickly. The planes would descend from the sky suddenly, one after the other, and drop their bombs. Then they would circle around and come back again, flying low and opening fire with their machine guns to mow down anyone still standing. Most often the only people left were the dead and the dying.

Elaine and Keith quickly learned to decipher the sounds of an oncoming attack. They would run with their parents to attempt to find safety. There was death in those sounds—death from the bombs, death from the shrapnel, death from the machine guns. If a person survived a falling bomb, there was still the concussion[93] from the blast. In order to depressurize and prevent concussion, the children would immediately cover their ears and open their mouths as they had been taught.

Mitter, in his book *Forgotten Ally*, described the sensation when a bomb explodes.

---

[93] When a bomb explodes, the blast produces an increase in atmospheric pressure, which can cause abdominal hemorrhage, lung injuries, perforation of the ear drum, concussion and traumatic brain injury—and possible death. In pregnant women, as with Florence, there was the serious risk of placenta detachment and hemorrhage.

People feel "a very strange wind" which foreshadows the impact to come. After a bomb is released from the aircraft's fuselage, it creates an airstream that forces its way into every empty space. People had to be very careful: if unprepared, the force of the pressure can throw them violently about. Then a person hears a noise "like the sky and the earth being smashed, like thunder in your head."[94]

Then in *Pleading China*, author Duncan McRoberts detailed one of his many bombing experiences.

Just as the morning sun dredged above the peaks of the distant mountains, flooding the plain with bright warm light, the weird drone of planes reached our ears. Together we raced towards the first building at the outskirts of a village just a short distance ahead. We had no sooner gained cover under its roof than the planes began releasing their demolition bombs. I had found shelter beneath a table and had no sooner sat down than a bomb struck the building. As the bomb exploded, the thick clay walls began to cave in. The concussion lifted me and threw me up against the toppling walls. It seemed as if every bone in my body would be crushed to pulp. Many people are killed by concussion alone. The vacuum following the explosion sucks all the air from their lungs, thus causing them to collapse. That bomb explosion blew my five fellow-workers to bits, and the concussion lifted portions of their bodies, flinging them under the table beside me. For five hours I lay covered with bits of the bodies of my five companions.[95]

If a person was not killed by an actual bomb, there was risk of being killed by the shrapnel from it. When a bomb explodes on impact, it leaves a hole in the ground and send sprays of steel several feet into the air extending for about one hundred feet around the bomb site.

In his first book, *While China Bleeds*, McRoberts described, with vivid imagery, more of the horrors of the bombing and strafing by Japanese pilots.

---

[94] Mitter, p. 177 (paraphrased).
[95] McRoberts (1946), pp. 66–67.

It was a very common sight to see old women dragging themselves along on their little bound[96] feet at a very slow speed. As they moved slowly along they cried out for help and pity but, alas, all were so intent upon saving their own lives that pity and help were not forthcoming. Even though one had the greatest desire to help, there were so many pitiable cases that to render assistance was almost impossible. (p. 36)

Some of the sights of that day shall never be forgotten. There were men so terribly wounded and maimed that it was impossible for them to walk, and they dragged themselves along on their bellies. Some of them had lost both legs while others were trailing one or two limbs held to their bodies by nothing more than small pieces of flesh, skin and bits of dirty clothing. (p.40)

I was alive, yet miserably satisfied to feel that I was only just alive. Thirst, starvation, body aches and mental strain all combined to force the cry from an aching throat over a much too swollen tongue and out through parched lips, "Oh, God, why don't you take me home to be with yourself?"

Every nerve in my body shrieked to God for deliverance from what I felt was too much for mere flesh and blood—the heavy drone of planes; the terrifying sound of ships power-diving; the whistle and loud explosion of death-dealing bombs; the monotonous rattle of machine-gun fire; the persistent attempts on the part of the enemy to crush hope and create terror in the hearts of brave men; the heart-rending scenes of anguish and suffering. The continual sight of blood, clear red or dried black, and its repulsive odor as it flowed freely from mangled forms. (p. 115)

---

[96] Bound feet dated back to the 10th Century when a female child's feet would be bound in tight bandages to keep them as tiny as possible. Diminutive feet were considered exceptionally beautiful and the ultimate in sexual allure. For the most part, only wealthy families practiced the custom, as poor or peasant families needed their female children to do heavy work in the fields and not be handicapped in this manner. Normally the procedure would start when a girl was about three years old. First, the feet would be soaked in warm water and then strips of thick wet cloth would be wound around each foot so that the four small toes and the front of the foot would be bent back beneath the sole of the foot. This procedure was repeated continually. The old bandages would be removed and the feet and legs massaged to help with circulation. Then the feet would be soaked in warm water again and rewrapped, with each wrapping being tighter than the one before. The entire process took about ten years as the bones had to be broken carefully and bent slowly. Even when the ideal shape was achieved, where the toes of the feet curled around the sole of the foot and touched the heel, the feet still had to be wrapped to maintain their shape. The end result was feet sometimes as small as three inches. Despite their perceived beauty, bound feet had limited function. Standing on them was painful and walking, virtually on the heels and knuckles of the toes, was excruciating, and the women would hobble along slowly and in an ungainly manner. By the time Clifford arrived in China, the practice had been virtually discontinued, although old women with bound feet were still a common sight.

Those refugees who survived the bombings would quickly remove the clothes from the dead and carry on with their journey. Sometimes a person did not even have to be dead to be relieved of their garments. Other refugees were found discarding items they had carried from home but now were too heavy to cart any farther—including their babies. The elderly were also left behind if they could not keep up the pace.

Elaine and Keith had already been traumatized by the bombing in Shangjao, and by being shot at during their flight to Shaowu. Elaine had also experienced the executions of young men fleeing into the hills to avoid being conscripted into the Nationalist Army.[97] Now they were experiencing more bombing and strafing and death that permeated the countryside. Even in her old age, Elaine still remembered blood running down the streets in the towns they travelled through. With their senses heightened, the children became unusually quiet and stayed close to their parents. They were tired and hungry and were looking emaciated and malnourished. Like their parents, their strength was diminishing rapidly and all of them were suffering from malaria.[98] But the family had no medication and no time to search out a doctor along the way. It was only when they were back in Canada that they were finally able to receive treatment.

The mental strain also wore on the family. It frayed their nerves and set them on edge, sapping them of vital strength. The strain threatened to displace the presence of faith and the confidence in God they felt in their lives, replacing such things with uncontrollable fear.

Although everyone in the family spoke Chinese, theirs was the dialect of east central China, whereas different dialects were spoken in different parts of the country. As the family travelled westward the dialects became more and more difficult to understand. This posed certain problems with communication, but not as much as if they did not speak any Chinese. And of

---

[97] Each household in a village had to provide one male to serve in the Army.

[98] Malaria is a common malady of China. It is transmitted by mosquitoes and, once contracted, is a life-long condition with periodic flare-ups of fever, chills and muscle aches. Sometimes temperatures reach as high as 104°F. When the flare-up subsides the person is left in a weakened state. Severe or recurring cases can cause kidney failure, seizures and death. Malaria is particularly dangerous in children and pregnant women. Before, when Florence experienced a flare-up, she would consult a Chinese doctor who would wrap various herbs in a cloth on the inside of her wrist close to the extruding blood vessels and, in a day or so, she would feel better. Western medicine uses a drug called Quinine to treat malaria.

course, Clifford and Florence could still converse through the standardized written language.

Finally, the young family arrived in Kweilin. It was the fall, the sunny dry season of the year. Although the Japanese controlled parts of the country north of the city, Kweilin was in Kwangsi Province, just beyond the reach of Japanese ground penetration. It was an ancient, exotic city, with a number of European-styled buildings situated in an agriculturally rich valley dominated by rice paddies and karst formations. These large conical-shaped formations or mountains were made of limestone, dolomite, and gypsum—all soluble rocks. For centuries they had been painted by Chinese artists for their beauty and uniqueness.

Kweilin was the capital city of Kwangsi and an important military and transport centre. One of China's three air force bases was located there. Another was situated at Kunming, and a third at Chungking, the wartime capital of China. The bases had been set up to protect the capital and other major cities from Japanese aerial attack, as well as to carry out strikes against Japanese forces in occupied China. The three bases formed a triangle, with Chungking at the apex, Kweilin at the southeast corner, and Kunming, four hundred miles to the west.

Kweilin was also the temporary home for numerous refugees fleeing from the Japanese-occupying forces. From a prewar population of seventy thousand, the city had grown to almost 500,000 by 1942. The city was not properly equipped for such a massive influx of people, as such accommodations were scarce. Some found shelter in the large water-worn caves on the outskirts of Kweilin while others built shanty houses of bamboo and mud, giving the city a rather slovenly, unkempt appearance.

Kweilin was a prime target for Japanese bombing runs and was continually under attack. Besides destroying valuable infrastructure and leaving large craters in the ground, the bombs started numerous fires that destroyed surrounding buildings and homes. Constructed of dried bamboo and wood, the buildings caught fire quickly. The only way to quench the flames was with hand pumps and bucket brigades. But these methods were virtually ineffective, and smoke and fire killed as many people or more than the actual bombs. In commenting on the devastation, Claire Chennault, the American commander of the Chinese Air Force, stated, "I waded through the rubble of bomb-battered ruins, smelled the sickeningly sweet stench of corpses rotting in wreckage and choked on the smoke" of the burning city.[99] With the continual bombing, famine settled in and food became scarce, so much so that stray dogs and rats were consumed until even their numbers became limited. Within the year, Kweilin fell to the Japanese.

Because of the refugee crisis and famine, the Paulsons rested only a short while in Kweilin before moving on to Kunming, four hundred miles away in Yunnan Province. They would not have to worry about Japanese patrols on this part of their journey, only continued bombing and strafing along the roadways. Transportation was also easier and bus travel was available, except there was no one bus that travelled from Kweilin to Kunming—a series of buses had to be taken. Starting from one town, they would ride the bus to the next stop, then get off and find another bus going in their direction. Because of the war, bus schedules were interrupted and a person never knew when the next bus would come, if at all. Sometimes they were able to get a ride on a truck or wagon passing by.

Buses in China were very uncomfortable and the rough roads made them even more so. But there was never any shortage of passengers—buses were always full, even overcrowded. As many people who could be crammed in were, including whatever each person was carrying. Every space was utilized and there were always people riding on top of the bus and hanging on to the back and sides.

Any form of transport was a target for Japanese attack. It did not matter if it was a military, commercial, or civilian vehicle, all came under fire. If planes were sighted or even heard in the sky, a bus would suddenly stop and everyone would scramble out to seek whatever shelter they could find. If there was no shelter, they would lie prone in ditches or fields. When it was safe, anyone still alive would run back to the bus, if it was still there to run to. More often than not, it was destroyed, with only a misshapen wreck of metal and debris left in its wake. Travel would then continue on foot.

Nearing Kunming, the family caught a ride on an American army truck. They rode in the back with supplies, completely exposed to the elements. Time passed slowly as the truck rumbled along. The road was rough and deeply creviced with ruts and potholes that jarred the passengers. The truck followed the road, winding this way and that, travelling up and down small hills as it

---

[99] Chennault, p. 89.

rocked side to side, the passengers echoing this motion. Everyone clung to something so as not to topple over. The children, being much smaller and lighter than their parents, were constantly being thrown about, first smashed against one side of the truck bed and then the other. All were covered in light brown dust churned up by the truck. Breathing was difficult.

The jostling of the truck proved hardest on Florence, and she suffered a miscarriage as a result. Of course, her weakened condition and impoverished diet also contributed to the loss. The small, not-quite-formed child was a little girl. Along with her grief, Florence also had to contend with physical complications and blood loss. In a nearby field the couple solemnly buried the little one that God had given them but had not allowed them to keep. Knowing that they would meet again in Heaven, and still having three little ones to shepherd, they pressed on.

Finally they arrived at Kunming. It was an ancient, walled city with narrow cobbled streets, built on a six thousand-foot plateau. Situated on the Chinese side of the Himalayas, it was surrounded by mountains to the north, east, and west. Various mountain tribespeople congregated there to sell their goods, buy supplies, and access medical services.

During WWII, Kunming was an important military centre, designated to be the nationalist's headquarters should the government at Chungking fall. One of China's three air force bases was there. Like Kweilin, Kunming was crowded with refugees, despite it being bombed continually. The CIM had a mission home there operated by Mr. and Mrs. Harrison, and the family was able to rest with them until they could arrange for a flight out of China. The rest was well needed as Clifford, Florence, and their three young children had walked—apart from the occasional ride on various transport vehicles—over one thousand miles across the whole of China, from Shaowu in the east to Kunming in the west.

Their oldest child, Philip, remained in China, a prisoner of the Japanese Army at Weihsien.

XXIII

Travel Home to Canada

On Christ, the solid Rock, I stand;
All other ground is sinking sand,
All other ground is sinking sand.[100]

In a relatively short period of time, Clifford was able to secure passage on an American army plane flying to India. It was a routine but perilous flight. Not only was there inclement weather to deal with but also the risk of attack from Japanese fighter planes. The force and direction of the winds over the Himalayan Mountains changed constantly and suddenly. One hour the wind would be blowing in one direction, the next hour in the opposite. Pilots of overburdened transport planes had to be on high alert to avoid being sucked into the side of a mountain. In describing the perils, Morse wrote:

> . . . the mountain ridges rise in wave after wave, each cresting higher than the one before . . . and the peaks are often shrouded in cloud or frosted with snow. Winds sweeping up all the way from the Indian Ocean break against these ridges and swoop down into the valleys and up again in draughts that create extreme atmospheric turbulence. This region is the dreaded "Hump" that so many American pilots had to cross in World War II. Their wheezing cargo planes could not climb over the thirteen-thousand-foot peaks of the ridge between India and Burma, so they had to seek out the gaps, few of them lower than nine thousand feet. Not surprisingly, some two thousand planes crashed against the mountain flanks during that desperate effort to supply China by air. (p. 21)

---

100 Hymn titled, "The Solid Rock," written by Edward Mote in the early 1800s.

The military planes fared slightly better in that they could take a more direct route over the mountains, but that meant having to fly at 23,000 feet. Despite the high altitude, attack by Japanese war planes was still a possibility. During the Paulsons' flight, their plane was shot at before it could hide out of sight in the mountain peaks.

The plane was unheated and bitterly cold inside. The family wore only light clothing and were chilled to the bone. The strong winds and vicious downdrafts tossed the plane around, jerking the passengers about in their seats and making them sick. The decreased level of oxygen at such a high altitude made it difficult to breathe, causing dizziness and headaches. Oxygen tanks and masks were available, but when the oxygen ran out, unconsciousness slipped in. Above 26,000 feet a person will die without oxygen; mountaineers call it the "death zone."

Eight hours later, after a tiresome and turbulent flight, the plane finally reached northern India. It had stopped briefly in Assam[101] before continuing on to Calcutta. Calcutta, like other cities in India, was densely populated and crowded, but now more so with large numbers of refugees seeking asylum there.

India was a welcome respite, offering safety from Japanese attack, sanitary conditions, and more nutritious food. In a newspaper interview with Florence after she had returned to Canada, it was reported that:

> Their greatest wonder on getting out of China into India was the amazing abundance of food. (According to Florence they had not) "seen butter for years and the milk . . . was extracted from the soy bean."[102]

> It was good to get to India where we could get something good to eat. In China food was so high-priced on account of inflation and so difficult to get on account of lack of transportation that eating was a problem.[103]

Clifford reported that:

> Conditions there were much better than in China. . . . We got clean beds, good train service, and were much impressed with what the British have done in India.[104]

---

[101] Assam was the Allied headquarters for northern India and Burma.
[102] The *Lethbridge Herald*, September 19, 1944, p. 6.
[103] The *Lethbridge Herald*, November 28, 1944, p. 8.
[104] The *Lethbridge Herald*, April 1, 1944, p. 9.

World War II was still in full operation. Only military planes were landing in Calcutta, and only military planes were leaving. Travel by ship was impossible, as the Japanese Navy regularly patrolled the Bay of Bengal. Transport to North America was best secured from Bombay, so Clifford and the family travelled there by train in the hopes of securing passage home. Anyone who was fortunate enough to secure transportation had to take whatever was available, not to mention whoever was willing to take passengers. This meant it would have to be either a military or cargo plane or ship. In the midst of a war, there were no passenger ships. After two months in India, Clifford was finally able to secure space on an American warship travelling back to the United States.

The quarters on board were cramped and all the portholes were covered with black curtains. The rules were strict and strictly enforced. Elaine, then seven, remembered one man going on deck and lighting a cigarette and promptly being placed in the brig for the remainder of the voyage. The Navy could not take any chances—a match or a glowing cigarette might be visible to a submarine if lurking on or near the surface of the water. The ship and the lives of the sailors on board depended on all rules being followed at all times.

This strictness was well emphasized by Isobel Kuhn who, in October of 1944, also headed to North America in a military warship, along with her husband and young son.

> Shortly after boarding, we mothers were summoned before a ship's officer for a lecture. He had probably been ordered to put fear into us, for he certainly tried his best. He told us that we were allowed on board only out of charity. This was not a passenger ship and there was no accommodation for babies. There was no baby food on board so we need not ask for it. There was no deck on the whole ship which was safe for babies—some had no railings and all had big uncovered hawse-holes through which a child could easily fall. "If your child falls overboard, the ship will not stop to pick it up. I tell you now, so you need not ask! It is up to each mother to watch her own child," he shouted to us. There was no laundry room for us, just the usual washbowls. We were to eat at officers' mess but that compelled two sittings, so that each meal must be finished within half an hour. We must line up ahead of time so as not to lose a minute in getting seated. And so on. When he finished there was

not one of us who would have dared to ask a favour, which was probably his purpose.[105]

Of course the food on board ship was plentiful and filling. It was the sustenance of Navy men, and the family was able to eat even better than they had in India. But their stomachs were not fully prepared for the heartiness of the food after trekking across China on starvation fare. They could only eat small amounts at a time and were often nauseated and sick to their stomachs.

Leaving Bombay, the warship travelled first through the Arabian Sea and then the Indian Ocean on its path toward Australia before proceeding to Los Angeles. To avoid detection from enemy submarines, the ship had to traverse the ocean in a criss-cross pattern—the zig-zag movements prevented submarines from getting an exact bearing on the ship and firing their torpedoes. Frequent and unpredictable changes of course meant, if a torpedo was fired, the ship might have already shifted direction and the shot would miss. However, constant pivoting meant a longer distance to travel and more time spent in the water. This increased the ship's vulnerability and used up considerably more fuel.

Despite all their ordeals and hardships, Clifford's and Florence's minds remained focused on Christ, who had led them safely to China and was now leading them safely home. Their belief that God was in control prevented any anxiety or worry from creeping into their thoughts. Even now, with the dangers at sea, Clifford's mind still turned to the Christ of his salvation, which he wrote about when he viewed the Southern Cross in the waters off the coast of Australia.

The Southern Cross

This time in crossing by ship from India to Canada, we were forced to take a rather circuitous route and travel right south around the southern tip of Australia in order to get out of Japanese submarine infested waters. And at one part of the journey we were nearly two days South of the Southern-most tip of Australia, which necessitated our travelling North in order to touch, for a few days, the port of Melbourne. Naturally, we were very interested to get a glimpse of that very common constellation in the Southern hemisphere known as the Southern Cross. One of the crew members on the ship one day mentioned to us that we were then

---

[105] Kuhn (1997), p. 145.

travelling in the vicinity where the Southern Cross was clearly visible at night. Being permitted to spend a time on the top deck that evening, we saw what we thought was the Southern Cross—there it lay well above the horizon to the right of our ship as we ploughed along, the stars of the cluster forming what looked like a cross. And the next day we happily remarked to one of the sailors that we had seen the Cross. Then he began to question us, "What time did you see it, and where did you see it?" So we told him that we had seen it hanging above the horizon off to the right.

And then the sailor said to us, "That which you saw far above the horizon was the false cross. There are two crosses—a true and a false. Most folks make the same mistake which you have made. The real Southern Cross is much lower and closer to the horizon. Tonight, you take another look, but this time look near the horizon, in fact the lower corner star seems to almost dip into the very water at the horizon. That is the true Southern Cross. There are two crosses, a true and a false."

And sure enough, when we went out the next night to again take a careful look at the sky, there hung the true Southern Cross, as the sailor had said, low down and hugging the horizon, in a slanting position and with the left corner star seeming to dip into the very water. We wondered that we had been so stupid to miss it the first evening. Yes, a true cross and a false one. Beware, my friend, of the false cross in our land with no mention of the atoning work of Christ for your sin and my sin upon Calvary.

Throughout the voyage, the ship's crew were on the lookout for enemy attack from the air as well as the sea. The ship's radioman constantly monitored the sonar,[106] listening to its monotonous ping for the distinctive variation in pitch that would indicate a submarine was nearby. Other crew members manned the lookout stations, ever vigilant for the sight or sound of a plane or surfaced submarine. Alertness was key. A submarine would never surface for more than thirty seconds, and then would never have more than a foot or two of periscope showing.

---

106 Sonar uses sound waves to detect objects under water by emitting ultrasonic waves into the water and monitoring the reflected echoes. It can detect the presence of a submarine and any change in its course and approximate distance away. Despite its sensitivity, it cannot ascertain a submarine's depth or distance at very long or very short ranges of three hundred yards or less. Nor can it be used if a ship's speed is more than twelve knots, or for several minutes after a depth charge has been released.

For the most part, the voyage was relatively uneventful until two days out of Los Angeles, when the ship's sonar sounded the distinctive ping of a submarine. The radioman quickly ascertained the sub's bearing and range. It was close by and closing to within striking distance. The fact that it carried some twenty-two torpedoes and was highly manoeuvrable—it was able to move quickly and in any direction, with a small turning ratio—made it a formidable enemy. The radioman promptly alerted the captain, who then sounded the alarm for the crew to man their respective battle stations. Though a warship, its mission was not an offensive one but simply a return to base. Their destination was Los Angeles, and their goal was to arrive there safely. If attacked, all they could do was defend themselves. The guns on deck would be of no use—if a submarine was under only three feet of water, it would be protected from the ship's artillery. And for a depth charge[107] to be effective in maiming or destroying a submarine, the explosion would have to be within ninety feet of it. Of course the ship, being faster, could outrun a submerged submarine, but there remained the risk of a second submarine farther ahead. The captain had to consider all possibilities. Anxiety was at a peak for the officers, the crew, and the passengers.

The captain decided to take evasive action, but just as the order was given, sonar detected that several torpedoes had already been fired. The only hope for the ship and the lives on board was to turn the ship parallel to the path of the torpedo and order maximum speed. By the grace of God, none of the torpedoes found their mark, although one came within a few feet of the vessel. Clifford's only reference to this terrifying incident was provided in an interview upon his return to Canada. He stated simply that "several days off the coast our ship was attacked by a submarine and narrowly missed being sunk."[108]

After journeying for forty-five days, the ship finally docked in Los Angeles. Being citizens of Canada and it still being war time, it took a while for the Paulsons to be processed through customs. All three children had been born in China and were not registered in Canada. Fortunately, people were there from the mission and the Red Cross to help them make whatever

---

[107] A depth charge is a bomb designed to explode under water at a specified depth. The shock wave or pressure created is sufficient to crush a submarine's hull.

[108] Although Clifford did not elaborate on the actual submarine attack, the sequence of events and description can be deduced from similar encounters in WWII.

arrangements were necessary. All family members were thin and emaciated. According to a newspaper article:

> Mr. Paulson, severely ill with malaria which he contracted seven years ago, stayed for several weeks in a rest home (at Huntington Park) in California, then spent 3 weeks in Vancouver with his parents.[109]

Although the family was able to rest and recuperate from their travels, the adjustment was difficult for all of them. The two younger children could not speak English, only Chinese, and were unaccustomed to Western food. Everything in China was served hot, so when they had their first taste of ice cream, they described it as "too hot" and as burning their mouths. They had never seen snow either. But like most children, they adjusted quickly to their new circumstances. In an interview with Madeleine Levason titled "Missionary, Family Return Home After Service, Suffering in China," Ms. Levason reported that the three Paulson children

> . . . are delighted with Canada which is like a dreamland to them. All children speak Chinese fluently and also picked up some Indian dialects during their stay in India. They are now learning to speak English rapidly.[110]

Adjustment for Clifford and Florence also meant dealing with the criticisms for having left Philip behind in China. I am certain that Clifford, in his own mind at least, answered, "But I left him in God's hands. What is better than that?" Actually, it is rather presumptuous to think that parents can protect or care for their children better than God. Clifford was particularly annoyed with several newspapers for the misinformation and derogatory portrayal of Asian people, which left him very cautious when giving interviews.

Upon the family's return to Canada, Clifford's first piece of business was to phone the Canadian government in Ottawa, to attempt to secure Philip's release from Weihsien. Next, he contacted the CIM offices in Toronto for funds, as the family had no money—their only possessions were the clothes on their backs. Treatment for malaria, from which they all suffered, was also a priority. Because Clifford's eyes had been affected by malaria and the bright sun, he had to wear sunglasses. After three weeks in Vancouver spent visiting

---

109 The *Lethbridge Herald*, April 1, 1944, p. 9.
110 Newspaper article; source unknown but recorded as written.

Clifford's parents, Florence took Blake to Chemanus on Vancouver Island to visit her mother while Clifford took Elaine and Keith with him to Edmonton to visit family there.

Various newspaper articles detailed some of the family's history and events in China.

Rev. Clifford T. Paulson, Back In Alberta, Tells of Escape From Japs[111]

. . . Rev. Clifford T. Paulson is back in Edmonton after 10 years with a mission in China.

But his son, 10-year-old Philip, did not return. He is a Japanese prisoner-of-war, interned when war was declared between Canada and Japan. Attending school in Shantung province, China, hundreds of miles away from the China Inland Mission station at Shangjao, province of Kiangsi China, where his parents lived, Philip was cut off by the events of war.

"We couldn't get him" Mr. Paulson explained. "If I had crossed the lines into Japanese-occupied territory, I would have been taken prisoner of war too and separated both from Philip and from my own family. There was no means of communication with him" . . . .

Meanwhile the family was awaiting word of possible repatriation of Philip from the east. Mr. Paulson has written the Canadian government requesting immediate action, but has had no answer yet. Now on 14 months furlough the missionary "may go back to China, if economic conditions there improve."

Missionary Tells of Life in China Under Japs—And After Pearl Harbor[112]

Back in Canada after nine and a half years of missionary work in China, her ten-year-old eldest son still at Weihsien in the hands of the Japanese, that is the situation of Mrs. C. T. Paulson, now visiting in Lethbridge with her sister, Mrs. Alex Harper.

Mrs. Paulson left Canada with her husband (in 1934) to serve in a non-sectarian mission station . . . in China. With them was their eldest

---

[111] The *Lethbridge Herald*, April 1, 1944, p. 9.
[112] The *Lethbridge Herald*, November 28, 1944, p. 8.

child, then 10 months old. Three other children were born in China and these returned with their parents to Alberta. Mrs. Paulson does not worry about the little boy who was left behind. "We know he is in good hands," she says. "Some of our own missionaries who are prisoners are looking after him and we have heard from time to time. Last time we heard was last January." The boy had been sent to school on the coast at the age of six and since then they have not seen him. The two missionaries with their three children have taken a house at Three Hills, Alberta, where they will spend the winter, and plan to return to their work in China as soon as it is possible.

Nine Months Under Japs

The Paulsons spent nine months in their station at Yangchow under domination of the Japs before Pearl Harbor. They had liberty of action to continue with their evangelistic work, conducting their Bible school and preaching in the streets. The mission was inspected weekly by the Japanese, who came in Chinese clothing for fear of snipers. Everything was subject to search.

After Pearl Harbor things changed for the missionaries. The Paulsons have spent some time in many parts of south China, being forced to flee from one place in 1942 on foot for nine days in a flooded area. That time they lost all their possessions except those they could carry. They spent five months at headquarters of the 3rd war army of China and Mr. Paulson saw General Doolittle and his men when they landed from the famous Tokyo raid.

The missions were frequently bombed and Mrs. Paulson says her children are still nervous from the effects. She loves the Chinese, calling them a pleasant people and remarking that they will do anything for one who smiles. The women and children of the missionaries wore Chinese clothing, padded in winter to protect them from the cold. They ate Chinese food too with chopsticks, even the children.

"It was good to get to India where we could get something good to eat," said Mrs. Paulson when asked if she had not been glad to get away. In China food was so high-priced on account of inflation and so difficult to get on account of lack of transportation that eating was a problem. Until they left China the Paulsons had not seen butter for three years and there was no sugar—only a kind of molasses made from sugar cane.

The journey home to Canada took many weeks, embracing most of the methods of travel from walking to flying, the missionaries landing in Vancouver finally on the last day of February this year.

All in all, Clifford and the family had lived nine-and-a-half years in China, and at no time had they experienced a day without war. Then, in leaving China, they had walked through the Valley of the Shadow of Death—the shadows of spiritual defeat, of illness, of starvation and thirst, and of enemy attack.

Yea, though I walk through the valley of the shadow of death, I will fear no evil: for thou art with me; thy rod and thy staff they comfort me.[113]

And the Lord who had said "lo, I am with you always"[114] saw them through.

When the eight-year Japanese-China war ended, an estimated 14 to 20 million Chinese were dead[115]—killed by Japanese bombing, war crimes, starvation, and combat.

---

[113] Psalm 23:4.
[114] Matthew 28:20.
[115] Mitter, p. 363.

XXIV

Ministry at PBI

No man that warreth entangleth himself with the affairs of this life;
that he may please Him who hath chosen him to be a soldier.

(II TIMOTHY 2:4)

After his return to Canada, Clifford joined the staff of Prairie Bible Institute in Three Hills, Alberta. He served as a Bible instructor there, from 1944 to 1952, and taught missions and homeletics, as well as the Old Testament books of Jeremiah and Daniel. He also served as associate editor of their magazine, the *Prairie Overcomer.*

Prairie Bible Institute was completely financed by voluntary contributions, nominal tuition fees, and room-and-board costs by the students. The students also helped defray expenses by completing various operational tasks, including setting tables, washing dishes, cooking, cleaning classrooms, shovelling snow, and maintaining the grounds. Additional volunteer manpower was provided by the surrounding communities. The institute had its own vegetable gardens, milk herd, and farmland, which provided sufficient food for the staff and students at minimal cost.

Staff members never received a salary, though they were provided with housing, utilities, food, and medical care. All work was considered voluntary and staff were employed on that basis. It was the sacrificial principle of unsalaried service. The school did not feel that offering an attractive salary would necessarily secure the best people for the work, meaning those of spiritual power and ability. In a PBI pamphlet titled *With God on the Prairies* appears the following statement: "Our simple principles of the laid-down life have screened out and kept from us many teachers and workers who might have proved an hindrance instead of a help to the work." (p. 40)

Prairie Bible Institute had a no-debt policy; the priority was to pay all expenses first from voluntary contributions before anything else. Whatever amount was left over was then divided equally among the staff members, from the president of the school down to the janitor. The usual monthly amount was somewhere between ten and fifteen dollars. The amount was not guaranteed and was solely dependent on monthly donations and expenses. Of course, Clifford tithed his usual monthly amount, which left even less of the stipend for a family of nine. Since the family had settled in Three Hills, three more children had been born—Lucille in 1945, Duane in 1949, and Marguerite in 1951.

Having heard of the unsalaried staff positions, the president of a large manufacturing company in the United States wrote a personal letter to the College:

> No person, not even an incompetent who could not get a teaching position anywhere else, would long continue to work for food, shelter, and less than fifteen dollars per month unless he were a truly consecrated individual who was working for Christ and the furtherance of His Kingdom . . .
>
> To me that can mean only one of two things. Either the staff at Prairie are completely consecrated, completely devout men and women—or they are crazy.
>
> Since you obviously could not continue to hold the interest of more than twelve hundred young men and women with a staff composed of crazy people, they must be devout Christians who are entirely willing to sacrifice the material things of this world for the cause of Almighty God and our Saviour, Jesus Christ.[116]

With PBI providing the basic necessities, personal expenses were kept to a minimum. The school owned the staff houses and allotted a monthly food credit to each staff member based on the number of heads in their family. Food trucks delivered milk and meat to each home daily; Mondays were liver delivery day. Additional food could be purchased at a low cost from a school-run grocery. The store also contained a room with big tables piled high with second-hand clothes from which the mothers could select what their children needed and what would fit them.

---

[116] Kirk, pp. 33–35.

Long after the family left Three Hills, the children were still wearing their second-hand clothing. Marguerite recalled the large navy blue bloomers that had been handed down from Elaine to Lucille and then to her, and being the only one in elementary school with such antiquated underwear. Although the clothes might have been old and out of style, they were always clean and mended, with Florence saving their precious dollars for regular dental care and new well-fitting shoes. Any medical care was typically provided by Florence after perusing a large medical book and implementing the recommended treatment. By worldly standards, denoted by possessions and money, the family was poor, but they were far richer than most by God's standards. It was like Hudson Taylor said when someone commented on his hand-to-mouth existence, "Yes, but it is from God's hand to my mouth."[117]

---

[117] Pollock, p. 98.

XXV

Reunion with Philip

The angel of the Lord encampeth round about them that fear him and delivereth them.

(PSALM 34:7)

When Clifford, Florence, and their three younger children left China, Philip was still interned at Weihsien. For him, life in camp remained the same day after day: chores, rules, school, lack of food, lack of warmth. Then in the summer of 1945, word came of a possible Japanese surrender. Excitement over the news was quickly tempered by the guards' threats: if Japan surrendered, they would first kill the internees and then kill themselves. Mixed with anticipation of the war's end, there was now the fear of execution. This fear became more real when it was later learned that the Japanese had executed Catholic priests and prisoners of war when the Philippines was liberated by the Allies. There was also the fear that the Japanese would simply stop all food supplies coming into the camp, leaving the residents to starve.

August 17, 1945, was just another routine day until the sound of a plane was heard flying low overhead. The name on the plane was visible from the ground: "The Flying Angel." Then someone yelled, "American plane! American plane!" Everywhere in the camp people stopped what they were doing and started cheering. As the plane circled the camp, seven soldiers parachuted out from it. The internees rushed for the front gate, which yielded easily to the mass of humanity pressing against it. Then the soldiers, surrounded by the internees, marched into camp and assumed control of the premises. One member of the team was Navy Lieutenant Jimmy Moore, a graduate of Chefoo School and the son of missionaries himself. He had specifically volunteered for the mission because of the missionary children at the camp.

A few days after the camp's liberation, B-29s dropped forty-four gallon drums of canned fruit nearby. The bombers had been converted from carrying bombs to carrying cargo that was dropped over the target area. Even with two parachutes, the cargo drums were exceedingly heavy, and many broke open when they hit the ground. When the all clear was given, Philip and the other children ran into the fields and consumed tin after tin of Del Monte peaches. Many of the food products were unknown to the children—they drank ketchup like they would any liquid and swallowed the chewing gum.

These deliveries continued several times a week for the next three to four weeks and included drums full of medicine, cigarettes, and clothing. Norman Cliff commented on the bounty, stating, "The years of bread porridge, bread pudding and bread-what-have-you were now over. . . . I recalled the words of the psalmist: 'Thou spreadest a table before me in the presence of mine enemies. My cup runneth over.'"[118]

In September 1945, the American military began processing the residents for evacuation, starting with the elderly and infirm. On September 25, Philip's group left the camp, travelling by lorry to Weihsien, then boarding a train to Tsingtao. As the train passed through the towns and countryside, numerous Chinese people lined their route, waving and cheering as the train passed through. A fellow Weihsien internee, Langdon Gilkey, recalled the Chinese people's sentiments.

> Perhaps the most moving aspect . . . was the sight of countless Chinese—farmers, merchants, peddlers, women, children—who lined the tracks in towns or ran from their fields in the countryside toward us, cheering and waving at the train as we passed.
>
> We were their allies; we had been captured by our common enemy; now our forces had defeated the hated invader of their country. They stood for hours to give us that momentary expression of their support as our train flashed past.[119]

In Shanghai the evacuees boarded an American troop ship, which transported them to San Francisco. From there, Philip travelled to Vancouver and then to Edmonton, where he met Clifford. The date was November 11, 1945; Philip was twelve. It had been over five years since he had seen his father.

---

[118] Cliff, p. 120.
[119] Gilkey, p. 224.

The Edmonton Journal.
Monday, November 12, 1945

Rev. Clifford T. Paulson, Three Hills, met his son Phillip, 12, Sunday night on the C.N.R. station platform here for the first time in five years and three months. At first neither father nor son recognized each other, as Phillip had been held by Japanese since the Chinese school he was attending was over-run before Pearl Harbor. Mr. Paulson, his wife and three other children fled their Chinese mission to the safety of India after the famous first Doolittle raid on Tokyo in 1942. The story of Mr. Paulson's part in aiding the daring American fliers when they crash-landed in China after the raid was told for the first time to THE EDMONTON JOURNAL.

Father Reunited With Son Freed From Jap Captivity

By Hal Pawson

Rev. Clifford Theodore Paulson, a tall, thin, fair man hustled down the C.N.R. platform Sunday night, his staring eyes searching for his son. Phillip Paulson, a small, thin, fair boy of 12, stood on the steps of an eastbound trans-continental train, his eyes searching for his father.

Father passed within four feet of son, and neither knew it—until an immediate woman relative recognized the bright neat boy as the nephew she had seen only as an infant. That brought father, a preacher and teacher at the Three Hills Prairie Bible school, and son, a prisoner of the Japanese in China since Pearl Harbor, together again for the first time in five years and three months.

It was a wordless reunion. It was a tearless reunion. Words and tears could not say what two smiles said when those two tumbled into each other's arms.

Those two smiles released an hitherto untold story of the Alberta missionary's part in the famous first raid on Tokyo by Gen. James Doolittle's American airmen on April 18, 1942.

The story of how Mr. Paulson played a human role in aiding American airmen returning from the raid, both dead and alive, remained until Sunday night a vital secret between the missionary and a few high Allied officials, Doolittle included. For on the story, told publicly for the first time to THE EDMONTON JOURNAL, balanced possible death of Phillip Paulson at the hands of the Japanese.

But let the history of the Paulsons, since Phillip was born in Innisfail in 1934, unfold itself in chronological order.

An infant of less than six months, Phillip left Innisfail with his parents for a mission in Kiangsi province, near Shangjao, in northern China. While there, Phillip's sister, Elaine, and two younger brothers, Keith and Blakely, were born. Only Elaine ever saw her brother as he was at school when the brothers were born.

Couldn't Reach Son

The school was the China Inland mission school, at Chefoo, Shantung province, several hundred miles from the Paulson's home mission. Before Pearl Harbor brought America and Canada to war with Japan, the Japanese overran Chefoo so suddenly that Mr. and Mrs. Paulson could not get their young son, then only six, out and to the safety of Kiangsi province in time.

"We weren't in a camp, but the Japanese guarded the school and kept us in there until Pearl Harbor," stated Phillip, matured, dignified, unabashed and well-mannered beyond his 12 years. "After Pearl Harbor they began taking over the school buildings one by one and we soon were moved to the North China camp at Weihsien."

"It was impossible to get through the Japanese lines to our boy," related Mr. Paulson. "Then in 1942 Gen. Doolittle raided Tokyo for the first time.

Americans Were Killed

"Many of the planes came back from Japan to Shangjao. The strips were not ready for them and most of the planes crashed attempting to land. Many American fliers were killed, others were hurt, and still others were dead as a result of the raid.

"I was the only white man in the entire district. Doolittle called me to his headquarters and for two days I was with him, arranging for the purchase of a burial field for the Americans, officiating at the many burial services and trying to gather the American dead.

"The Japanese found where the planes had landed and started a drive through Kiangsi province. They began overrunning Shangjao before I could complete my work. My family and I had to flee before their advance, leaving some American dead still lying along the roadsides.

Placed Son in Danger

"It was my duty to those Americans, yet it placed the life of my interned son in terrible jeopardy. Had the Japanese ever discovered my identity I believe my son would have been killed in reprisal. They knew a white man had helped the Americans, but this story was so well silenced that they never learned who that white man was. Now it does not matter. My son is home, safe and sound, thank God."

Knowing Phillip was a Japanese prisoner, the Paulsons were forced to flee before the advancing Japanese armies, through southern China, across Burma and into the safety of India. At the time of the long, perilous trek, Mr. Paulson was suffering from malaria, a malady which still strikes him periodically.

Mr. Paulson's ambition is to return to his missionary work in China. "If the way is ever cleared for me I shall return at once," he stated Sunday night.

Of his long internment by the Japanese, young Phillip said: "They did not treat us badly. The Chinese were more poorly treated. There were so many of them they could not be put in camps. We went to school all the time in camp, although we could not do as much as when we were in the mission school.

"Our happiest time was the day three days after the war ended that American planes dropped 250 parachutes of food to us and also dropped seven men—interpreters and such. From then until we started moving to Chindow and the boat that was taking us home they dropped food all the time. My, we ate like we hadn't for years.

"We used to get the news quickly. There was a Chinese who came in to clean the cesspools in the camp. He was a secret service man from Chungking and he gave us all the news. We knew as soon as the war was over. The people in the camp were all so happy that when the American planes came over we all ran out of the camp, and the Japs did not do anything.

Didn't Know Father

"I didn't know my father when I got here. I couldn't remember what he looked like. But it is posh to be home and see him again. I never saw my young brother Blakely before. Monday I will see mother and Elaine and Keith. It is so much. I also had a posh visit with my grandfather and grandmother (Mr. and Mrs. Benjamin Paulson) for two days in Vancouver.

"I didn't have any clothing when I started for home. We all came by boat, and when we stopped at Okinawa, a U.S. marine gave me an outfit. I had the little field cap, and they cut down the jacket and trousers. I got new clothing when we got to Los Angeles, but I'm keeping my marine suit. We were just out of Pearl Harbor on the boat when I had my 12th birthday."

Phillip was 1 1/2 months traveling from China to Vancouver. Only sad touch at the station Sunday night was when he said goodbye to his teacher, Miss Pearl Young, of Pictou, N.S., and nine other Canadian children.

Continued to Study

"Most of these children know no one but the people in the Weihsien camp," explained Miss Young. "I was their teacher at the inland mission school. The Japanese let us continue our studies, although the accommodations were poor. The food and sanitary facilities were poor, but there was no bad treatment. And the older people in the camp were good to the children. They even saw they had a better than fair share of the food. And they have been fed so well since we were liberated." Miss Young is conducting the party of nine children as far as Toronto. She will take her year's furlough at her home and then hopes to be allowed to return to China. When the party left China, there were 19 children from the school in it.

Mr. Paulson, Phillip and Blakely spent Sunday night at the Edmonton home of Mr. Paulson's sister, 11727 90 st. Monday, they left for Three Hills, where Phillip again will see his mother and meet his other brother and sister.

A dozen other relatives were at the C.N.R. station to greet him Sunday night. He cut a happily dignified figure in his short green heavy jacket and blue trousers as he formally acknowledged their acquaintance with handshakes and serious thoughtful answers to their questions.

Among those who greeted him was his 12-year-old cousin, Clifford Paulson, son of Mr. and Mrs. P. O. Paulson, 9111 88 ave. "Where did you get that English accent?" demanded Clifford in his hard Canadian drawl. "I was in an English school, you see," smiled back Phillip. "I'll have him talking Canadian in six months if I get the chance," Clifford stated later.

When Philip was in his thirties, he wrote a brief account of his life for the PBI's youth magazine, *Young Pilot*.[120]

CAPTURED!

By Philip Paulson

When I was a baby of only nine months, my parents sailed to China as missionaries of the Chine Inland Mission. Soon after we arrived, I was put into the care of a "Nana," so I would not hinder my parents' study of Chinese, a very difficult language.

I was now in a different world, an Oriental world, a world full of strange sights and sounds. My playmates were chubby little boys and girls with slanted eyes and coal-black hair, and dressed in padded clothes—quite different from the fair-haired, white-skinned children we had left behind.

My play world was different, too. I spent many happy hours sitting in one of two wicker baskets tied to the ends of a long bamboo pole, which was slung over the shoulder of a Chinese "coolie." Away we would go, laughing and singing as he trotted us around the compound, or downtown to the market.

But all is not play forever—schooldays must come; and so, at the age of six, I was sent hundreds of miles away to Chefoo, a Christian boarding school in northeastern China.

We were divided into three competitive groups: the House of Livingstone, the House of Carey, and the House of Stanley. The House of Livingston seldom came out on top, maybe because one of its members was, well—me!

In spite of the fact that we saw our families only during summer vacations, and occasionally at Christmas, those years at boarding school were good years. We grew to love our teachers, and to respect the awesome headmaster, who corrected our more serious misbehaviour. They admirably tried to take the place of our parents, teaching us both spiritually and intellectually.

I had been in Chefoo school for two years when the picture suddenly changed. The Japanese invaded China. All foreigners were put under arrest, and so we became prisoners in our own school premises. Japanese

[120] Issues March, 1965 (pp. 24, 30–31) and April, 1965 (pp. 29–31).

soldiers guarded us day and night, but allowed us to carry on with our necessary schoolwork.

After nine months of imprisonment at Chefoo, we were ordered to leave for Weishien Concentration Camp, some one hundred miles away. We could take with us only what we could carry in our hands.

At Weishien we were crowded with a thousand or more British and American civilians and servicemen into what was once a trade school. We students were assigned as many as twelve to a room. We laid our straw ticks out on the bare floor like a giant clock, so that our feet pointed to the filthy old pot-bellied stove in the centre of the room.

My shoes soon wore out, and I then had to go barefoot, in spite of the bitter cold. Many a day in those cold North China winters we were huddled around our old stove, scorching our legs when we got too close in our effort to keep warm.

With God's help, our teachers were able to instruct us, using the few textbooks they managed to carry with them from Chefoo. Just how much He did help us was proved to me later when, after the war, I was able to enter the same grade as others my age, in spite of missing so much school.

Sanitation and hygiene were poor, and medical help was very inadequate, but in spite of these and other hardships, life in camp was not always harsh. We as children did not mind too much our daily diet of watery soup, horse meat, and more soup. The Japanese guards liked children, and allowed us to hold their rifles, warning us against touching the razor-sharp bayonets on the ends of the rifles.

We enjoyed daily roll call, when everyone was ordered to line up and count off in Japanese: "ichi, nee, san, shi, go," and so on. If someone was missing, an immediate search was made, because escapes were not uncommon.

I vividly remember one early morning roll call. Two men were missing. A quick search by the guards on duty revealed a narrow tunnel leading from the floor of the missing prisoners' room. The guards followed it under and beyond the high stone wall which surrounded the camp. Where had the men gone? Had they been caught? Rumours were flying thick and fast, but we never heard of the men again.

One day something very sad occurred. Two or three of the older boys tried to see if they could get an electric shock by jumping up and lightly touching the electrified barbed wire that was strung around the top of the stone wall—"for kicks," in other words. As I was watching them, one of them made too strong a contact and was electrocuted on the spot. That death surely sobered us for a while.

All mail was withheld from us during our three-and-a-half years of internment; so I received no word from my parents, who had, unknown to me, miraculously escaped the invasion. They did not know for sure where or how I was. But the Lord protected me, and gave my parents grace to meet each new day. At that time I did not know the Lord, but He was taking care of me, and sparing my life for a purpose.

So the time went by, until one wonderful day which I cannot even fully remember. I must have been playing with some of the other fellows, for that was our greatest pastime. At any rate, the next thing I knew, the sky was alive with silvery B-29s. Suddenly parachutes of all sizes and colours tumbled out of airplane bomb bays and popped open, dangling beneath them barrels of much-needed food and clothing.

Our excitement mounted as we watched seven airmen parachute from one of the planes. When the Japanese guards saw that these men were coming to liberate us, they fled, probably knowing that it meant the war had ended. And that meant we were no longer prisoners!

Of course we lost no time in breaking open the crates and barrels, and it was then that I received my first candy bar and chewing gum. We ate powdered milk by the spoonful, and gorged ourselves on "K rations" (a chocolate bar with enough vitamins in each square for a full meal). Perhaps an even greater discovery was made when I found a pair of shoes, two sizes too big, but shiny and new enough to make me as proud as punch!

After years without the proper nourishment needed for healthy bodies, it took a few months for us to be built up again. When we were able, however, we were transported to Shanghai, where we boarded the troopship *U.S.S. La Vaca*. Along with five thousand marines who were picked up at Okinawa, we sailed for San Francisco and home. While on board the ship, we were assigned to bunks, which were stacked five high, the top one seeming to be only a foot from the ceiling. And—you guessed it—mine was the top one.

In San Francisco we were placed under the care of the Red Cross. We were again fed properly for a few weeks, given more clothes, and finally placed on trains to return to our homes. I needn't tell you how glad we all were to see our families again, although it all seemed so strange at first.

During those war years, many Christians had prayed for me, including a little girl in Saskatchewan, who later became my wife. Although God answered those prayers, He had to bring me through rougher waters before I was willing to yield my life to Him.

My parents were unable to return to China as missionaries, and so they served on the staff of Prairie Bible Institute at Three Hills, Alberta, Canada. During this time, I completed grades seven through eleven, and ended my high school training with a year of technical school in the city of Calgary.

After landing a fairly good job, I began to enjoy the things a big city has to offer, and, instead of turning my thoughts to Bible school and the mission field, I wanted to travel, to "see the world," to enjoy life. Even though I was the son of missionaries and had been brought up in a home that emphasized missions, I had no concern for others who did not know the Lord Jesus as their personal Saviour. My only concern was for my own enjoyment.

My "home" in Calgary at that time was a boarding house, where I lived with a half-dozen other fellows. One of them, a Scottish fellow, became my buddy. We had not been friends long when we decided to take a trip to Europe, Asia, Australia, and New Zealand. We figured we would need about one thousand dollars apiece if we could work and hitchhike along the way.

With these few plans, we made reservations on a Dutch ship, *The Great Bear.* Then for a whole year we scrimped and saved until our sailing day arrived. Armed with only our cameras and one suitcase each, we boarded our ship at Montreal, and settled into our cabin.

It was spring, and the crossing was rough—so rough that at times even the upper decks were lashed with the spray from thirty-foot waves. In spite of the heavy seas, we finally arrived at Rotterdam, Holland, in good shape, and our real adventures began.

From Holland we hitchhiked through most of the major countries of free Europe, crossed the Channel into England, and finally arrived at my friend's home in Scotland. For the next few months we stayed there with his folk.

Although I was enjoying my stay there in Scotland, I was anxious to be off again, and so, after working and sight-seeing in Britain for six months, I said good bye to my buddy, who could not continue the trip, and set sail for Australia and what was to be a turning point in my life.

At London, England, I boarded the *Oronsay* and stood alongside the rail watching four churning tugs push us slowly out from the dock. As the English coastline faded into the distance, I thought, "This is the life for me!" I was not yet twenty-one, and my life lay ahead of me. Everything looked rosy—I had a lot of time to live for the Lord later on. Right now I was going to enjoy life to the full!

Deep within, a strange little yearning, long buried beneath the clutter of self-ambition, stirred itself. It seemed to say, "You ought to be sailing to some foreign land as a missionary, instead of being out for a good time." But I wasn't a missionary in any sense of the word. I quickly turned my thoughts to other things to bury the bothersome little thought. After all, this was supposed to be a "joy ride," and I wanted to enjoy it!

The next five weeks were a maze of colourful sights and sounds. We stopped at such romantic places as Gibraltar, Port Said (which included a trip to the Sphinx and the Great Pyramid, near Cairo), Aden, Colombo, and all the principle cities of western and southern Australia.

Early in February we arrived at Sydney, Australia, where I soon found a good-paying job with an aluminum company. For four months I worked seven days a week, and finally had enough money saved to buy my ticket home, plus some left over to continue any travels.

After I quit my job, the centre of my world became Bondi Beach, perhaps the most famous of beaches next to Waikiki. The sunny summer days were filled with surfing, skin diving and sunbathing.

One day a group of us decided to go surfing, and so we headed for the beach. That day the surf was tops, and I took my board out as far as I could go. So great was my desire to know the thrill of riding that "big one," that I did not notice the undercurrent that was slowly drawing me away from the others.

Suddenly a huge wave hit me, and I lost my surfboard. I started to swim for it, but I found myself caught in a backwash. I struggled to release myself from its grip, but, no matter how hard I swam, the current just carried me back and forth, back and forth.

Once I looked up to try to find the others, but they were away off in the distance. Then I looked for the lifeguards. They were tiny specks on the beach, and all at once, I realized my danger. We had been warned to stay with the group, and now I found myself separated from the others, in shark-infested waters, and completely helpless!

In desperation I attempted again to break loose from the current, but my strength was giving out. And it was useless to try to call for help—no one could hear me, anyway.

I realized then that I was drowning, and I was scared. My thoughts and feelings during those frightful moments are impossible to describe.

My whole life flashed onto the picture screen of my mind. I saw the special meetings that had been held in our community when I was a lad of thirteen. I saw myself during those meetings asking the Lord Jesus into my heart. And I saw the years following—years that I had refused to give to my Lord. I had not prayed nor lived for Him. I had been careless and thoughtless, and, now that I needed Him, I did not know whether He would help me, or not. I was not even sure whether I would go to Heaven.

I had been in prison once, years ago, through no fault of my own. But now I was in a prison of my own making, with no one to look to for deliverance! My thoughts became my torture chamber, and at last I drifted into unconsciousness.

After some time I opened my eyes. A sea of tanned faces surged about me, and it took me awhile to realize what was happening. The faces finally acquired bodies, and proved to be a group of brawny lifeguards bending over me. Was I alive? I pinched myself all over to see. Yes, I was alive—the Lord had in love and mercy spared me.

Right there, in front of all those curious onlookers, I knelt down on the beach and quietly promised the Lord He could have my life.

The lifeguards later explained to me that they had seen me get drawn away in the current, and that two of them had snapped ropes around themselves and had swum after me. Once they had gotten hold of me, other guards on the beach had hauled us back by means of winches mounted on the beach.

With new purpose in life, I headed home—home to Christian friends and loved ones, who soon saw their prayers for me being answered.

I am happy to say that I have kept my promise to God made that day on my altar of sand; but how much better it would have been to have lived the other years for Him, too, instead of wasting them in worldly pleasure. Now I want to spend the rest of my time wisely, realizing that Christ may return at any moment and that I am His captive—for life!

XXVI

Missionary Colleagues: Exodus of the CIM

Fear thou not; for I am with thee: be not dismayed; for I am thy God: I will strengthen thee; yea, I will help thee; yea, I will uphold thee with the right hand of my righteousness.

(ISAIAH 41:10)

In 1949, the Communist Party and its forces emerged triumphant in the protracted civil war with the nationalist government. Chiang Kai-shek and his supporters fled to Taiwan, the communists established the People's Republic of China, and life began to change dramatically for the Chinese people and the foreigners in their midst.

First came the accusations, where anyone associated with the former government was denounced and then summarily executed. Rich landowners, businessmen, educators, and the intelligentsia, and simply anyone who did not support the new regime were also at risk. People attending these accusation meetings were required to make some kind of denunciation. If they were not sufficiently harsh or enthusiastic enough, they could draw unwanted attention to themselves. While attendance at accusation meetings was expected, attendance at the subsequent executions was often mandatory, even for very young school children.

House searches, usually at night, became commonplace, with numerous citizens being taken to party headquarters for interrogation. Most did not return. Political propaganda played constantly over public address systems and was enthusiastically proclaimed at indoctrination meetings in the evenings. Attendance at these meetings was compulsory. Although mission leaders were well aware of the antagonistic attitude of the communist government toward the Gospel, they reaffirmed their call to China whether under nationalist or communist rule. Even when other missions were pulling out of China and Americans were being urged by their consulates to leave, the CIM remained, reminding its members that "while we do not court danger, we are committed to a life which may involve it."[121] The one exception to staying was Alfred Bosshardt. In 1934, Alfred had been captured by communist soldiers and forced to march with them on an arduous journey across China. This was called the Long March. After 560 days of captivity and brutal treatment, he was released. The mission offered him the freedom to leave rather than live under communism. Alfred chose to stay.

Gradually, communist attention turned to the missionary. The first signs of trouble came in 1948, when Miss Lewell of the Swedish mission was suddenly arrested, tried as a criminal, and put to death. Her execution was completely unexpected as she had been living in a communist-controlled region for some time. Four more executions quickly followed—missionaries of different faiths living in different parts of the country.

Then in January 1951, the CIM reconsidered its decision to remain in China, having realized that their presence was putting the lives of Chinese Christians in danger. A complete evacuation was ordered. Phyllis Thompson called it "the reluctant exodus," in that it was not the actual desire of the missionaries to leave but the concerted effort of the communist government to force them out. Communism was atheistic and, as such, antithetical to Christianity. It considered missionaries to be Imperialist spies or agents of foreign governments. Like the Apostle Paul, when he was shipwrecked in the Great Sea,[122] the mission leaders prayed that all would be extricated safely. Fortunately, their numbers had been reduced in previous years, with members like the Paulsons and others on furlough or medical leave having left. At the beginning of 1951, 627 adults and several hundred children remained in China.

One particular prayer for the safe exodus of the missionaries was made by a Eurasian lady, Mrs. Mason, who lived at the mission home in Shanghai.

On one occasion, her mind was full of the menacing situation her fellow-missionaries in the interior faced. . . . The familiar records of the

---

[121] Thompson, p. 18.
[122] Acts 27.

Exodus impressed themselves on her. In particular, she thought of the steady, insistent command of God Himself when he sent word through Moses again and again to Pharaoh: "Let My people go!" The conflict had been long and fierce, but eventually the Enemy had collapsed in defeat. The children of Israel made their historic departure from Egypt. In that long record, one little phrase somehow fastened itself in Mrs. Mason's memory. "There shall not a hoof be left behind". . . .

Deeply moved, Mrs. Mason urgently pleaded for her beloved China Inland Mission and everyone in it. "Lord!" she prayed. "Bring them all out. Everyone. Let not a hoof—nor a husband—be left behind!". . . .

(The prayer) was relevant. The women and children would be sent out first. Some men would have to stay behind to clear up affairs before they could leave. What if one here, one there, were refused permission to go, if they were hauled before a People's Tribunal and sentenced to imprisonment, hard labor, or death?

In the months and years that followed, Mrs. Mason continued praying in the same words: "Lord, let not a hoof nor a husband be left behind."[123]

Having made the decision to evacuate all of its missionaries and their families, Headquarters' staff calculated that it would probably cost several hundred thousand dollars to do so. Not only was there the cost of travel out of China and back to the missionaries' home countries, as well as their living expenses, but also the additional cost of severance pay for the servants, some of whom demanded exorbitant sums as compensation for loss of employment.

At the time, the mission only had ten thousand dollars in their furlough account, which would only cover the cost for twenty people to leave. Additional monies could not even be obtained by the sale of mission properties, as most had been appropriated by the communist government. Regardless of their plight, plans went ahead for evacuation, with reliance on God to provide the necessary funds. Before, God had always met their needs, like when an unexpected gift of sixty thousand dollars had arrived at the close of WWII. That amount had been sufficient to meet the needs of the hundreds of CIM missionaries and children when they were suddenly released from the internment camps. And this time, God provided again. A communist organization approached the mission about renting their spacious

---

123 Thompson, pp. 90–91.

headquarters, paying several years' rent in advance. The sum covered the entire cost of the CIM's withdrawal from China.

Even though the communists wanted the missionaries gone, they made it difficult for them to leave.

> No one could go without an exit visa. It was not granted until the applicant could prove he was leaving behind no unpaid debts. This involved inserting a notice in the local paper, inviting anyone to whom he owed anything to produce the evidence, so that matters could be settled. To insert the notice in the paper, however, was not as simple as it sounded. Permission to do so at all had to be obtained from the authorities. When that was withheld, there was nothing to do but to wait. No explanation could be demanded.
>
> The most sinister demand made on those waiting to leave the country was that they must have personal guarantors who would stand surety for them even after they left. Each person leaving China was only permitted to do so because a Chinese citizen had promised to be responsible for any unpaid debts, any undisclosed crimes—and for anything the one who left might say or do that was detrimental to the People's Government of China when back in his own homeland.[124]

Furthermore, the applicant, and even the older children, had to document their personal life history, which was then subjected to official scrutiny and lengthy questioning. All personal belongings had to be registered, and any accusations against the person had to be investigated and dealt with before they could leave. If the allegation was found to be valid, which most often it was, the person would be charged and possibly imprisoned. Most often an exit permit took months or, in some cases, years to obtain.

Permission was actually required for everything—permission to travel within the country, permission to leave the country, and permission to sell belongings or even give them away. Prior to 1951, several missionaries were able to flee China before the restrictions set in. One was Isobel Kuhn,[125] a well-known CIM missionary and author who managed to escape over the treacherous mountains of northwest China and through the jungles of Upper Burma with her six-year-old son, Danny. Her husband, John, had been

124 Thompson, pp. 66–67.
125 Appendix H.

detained earlier in Paoshan, when the city was captured by communists. He was unable to leave.

Early in 1951, the mass exodus of missionaries began.

> They came by the tens and twenties, busloads and trainloads of them streaming across the little iron bridge over the ditch that passed for a creek, with barbed wire on either side, that separated Hong Kong . . . from "Red China." Some came running across, laughing and weeping and kissing the flag. Others were carried on litters, or hobbled on swollen limbs. Still others came handcuffed, prisoners to the end. On two days in March, one hundred children and teachers from the China Inland Mission Chefoo school came in double lines, each carrying their three most important possessions: Bible, passport, and toothbrush.[126]

By 1952, only two CIM missionaries remained in China—Dr. Rupert Clarke and Arthur Mathews.[127] Both were confined to their homes in Tsinghai Province, near the Tibetan border. Finally, in 1953, they were released, and Mrs. Mason's prayer was answered that "not a hoof nor a husband" would be left behind.

Since the decision had been made to withdraw from China, "not one member had died in China. Nor had any member emerged maimed. Not one had been left behind. There had been deaths in the mission by accident, by sudden heart attack, by normal illness and old age outside of China during those years, but none inside. All had come safely out."[128]

---

[126] Austin, p. 305.
[127] Appendix I.
[128] Thompson, p. 185.

XXVII

Death

In the Apostle Paul's epistle to the Philippians, he wrote:

> *For to me to live is Christ, and to die is gain.*
>
> *But if I live in the flesh, this is the fruit of my labour: yet what I shall choose I wot not.*
>
> *For I am in a strait betwixt two, having a desire to depart, and to be with Christ; which is far better:*
>
> *Nevertheless to abide in the flesh is more needful for you.*
>
> *And having this confidence, I know that I shall abide and continue with you all for your furtherance and joy of faith.*
>
> (PHILIPPIANS 1:21–25)

In commenting on the text, Clifford wrote:

> It is not frustration that prompts Paul's desire to shift his tent to the heavenly encampment. He is not disappointed or disillusioned with life, so completely "fed-up" that he has nothing else to live for. Far from it. He wants nothing out of life but to live Christ; and nothing out of death but to be with the Lord, "For to me to live is Christ, and to die is gain." Christ is the Sum-Total of all his desires. He aims to be all for Christ while he lives, to find Christ all for him when he dies. He has everything to live for; but he has also everything to die for.
>
> The believer's conception of death is described so beautifully in these two expressions, "To die is gain" and "To be with Christ which is far better." Death for the Christian is not a bereavement, it is a bequest. We do not lose, we gain. We part with our earthly life to enter into Christ's

heavenly life; we lay down our burdens to enjoy heavenly bliss; we leave our earthly friends to enter into the heavenly family. Death to the Christian is not a termination; it is a translation. When we die we do not pass to endless oblivion or fade away in undisturbed unconsciousness. We go to be with Christ. A far better life awaits us at the end of the road; a more gainful employment in "following the Lamb whithersoever He goeth" calls us.

No wonder Paul is in a "strait betwixt two"; the tug of his Father's Home seems irresistible. He wants to go Home; but a task remains to be done. He knows what is best for him, but what is best for his brethren prevails. In his bonds he is suffering for the furtherance of the Gospel; in his body he is staying for the believers' "furtherance and joy of faith."

Even our most legitimate desires, our highest spiritual hopes, must be surrendered in the service of others. "For Christ and souls" must ever be the deciding factor in any conflict between desire and duty. To live must be Christ, first, foremost and finally.

Only one life,
'Twill soon be past;
Only what's done
For Christ will last.[129]

Clifford died peacefully in the late morning hours of November 26, 1986; his wife of fifty-five years was at his bedside. He was seventy-nine.

---

[129] Written by C. T. Studd.

Appendix A

Genealogy

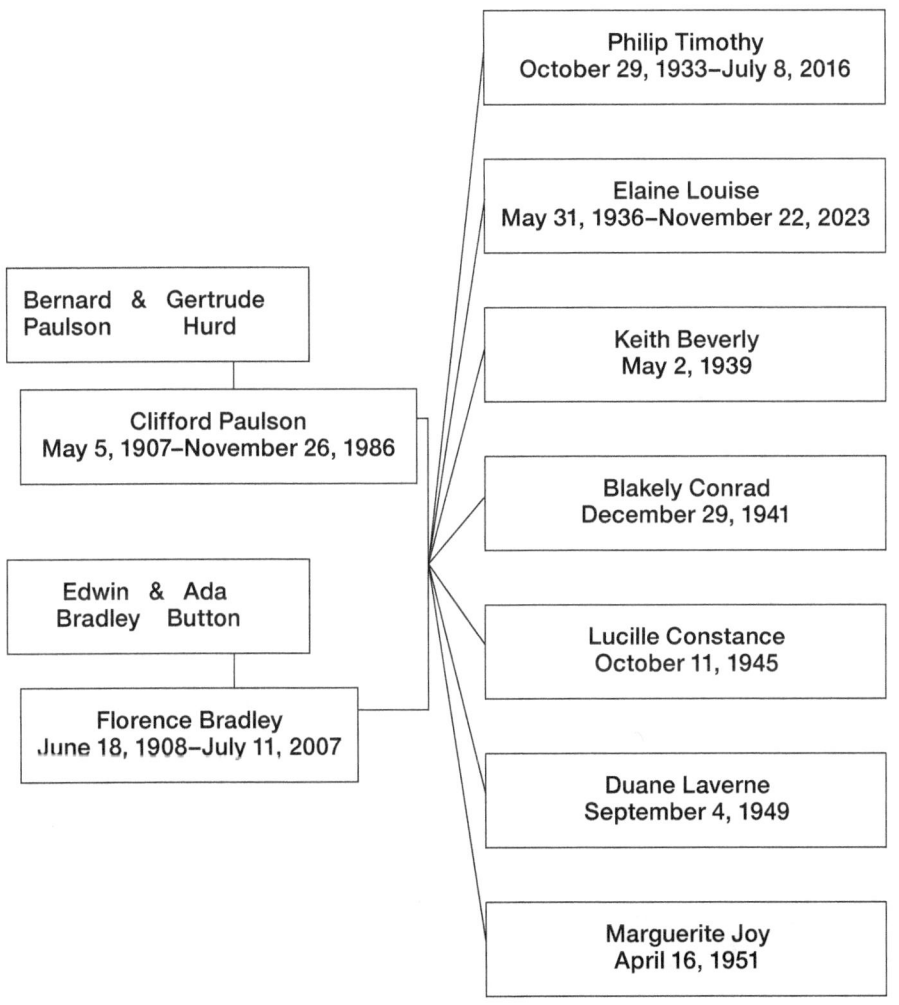

Bernard & Gertrude
Paulson   Hurd

Clifford Paulson
May 5, 1907–November 26, 1986

Edwin & Ada
Bradley   Button

Florence Bradley
June 18, 1908–July 11, 2007

Philip Timothy
October 29, 1933–July 8, 2016

Elaine Louise
May 31, 1936–November 22, 2023

Keith Beverly
May 2, 1939

Blakely Conrad
December 29, 1941

Lucille Constance
October 11, 1945

Duane Laverne
September 4, 1949

Marguerite Joy
April 16, 1951

Appendix B

Thy Brother's Blood Crieth

Amy Carmichael, an Irish missionary to India in the 1900s and the author of numerous books, also proclaimed the message of responsibility to reach the unsaved, published in the tract, "Thy Brother's Blood Crieth."

The tom-toms thumped straight on all night, and the darkness shuddered round me like a living, feeling thing, I could not go to sleep, so I lay awake and looked; and I saw, as it seemed, this:

That I stood on a grassy sward, and at my feet a precipice broke sheer down into infinite space. I looked, but saw no bottom; only cloud shapes, black and furiously coiled, and great shadow-shrouded hollows, and unfathomable depths. Back I drew, dizzy at the depth.

Then I saw forms of people moving single file along the grass. They were making for the edge. There was a woman with a baby in her arms and another little child holding on to her dress. She was on the very verge. Then I saw that she was blind. She lifted her foot for the next step . . . it trod air. She was over, and the children over with her. Oh, the cry as they went over!

Then I saw more streams of people flowing from all quarters. All were blind, stone blind; all made straight for the precipice edge. There were shrieks as they suddenly knew themselves falling, and a tossing up of helpless arms, catching, clutching at empty air. But some went over quietly, and fell without a sound.

Then I wondered, with a wonder that was simply agony, why no one stopped them at the edge. I could not. I was glued to the ground, and I could not call; though I strained and tried, only a whisper would come.

Then I saw that along the edge there were sentries set at intervals. But the intervals were too great; there were wide, unguarded gaps between. And over these gaps the people fell in their blindness, quite unwarned; and the green grass seemed blood-red to me, and the gulf yawned like the mouth of hell.

Then I saw, like a little picture of peace, a group of people under some trees with their backs turned towards the gulf. They were making daisy chains. Sometimes when a piercing shriek cut the quiet air and reached them, it disturbed them and they thought it a rather vulgar noise. And if one of their number started up and wanted to go and do something to help, then all the others would pull that one down. "Why should you get so excited about it? You must wait for a definite call to go! You haven't finished your daisy chain yet. It would be really selfish," they said, "to leave us to finish the work alone."

There was another group. It was made up of people whose great desire was to get more sentries out; but they found that very few wanted to go, and sometimes there were no sentries set for miles and miles of the edge.

Once a girl stood alone in her place, waving the people back; but her mother and other relations called, and reminded her that her furlough was due; she must not break the rules. And being tired and needing a change, she had to go and rest for awhile; but no one was sent to guard her gap, and over and over the people fell, like a waterfall of souls.

Once a child caught at a tuft of grass that grew at the very brink of the gulf; it clung convulsively, and it called—but nobody seemed to hear. Then the roots of the grass gave way, and with a cry the child went over, its two little hands still holding tight to the torn-off bunch of grass. And the girl who longed to be back in her gap thought she heard the little one cry, and she sprang up and wanted to go; at which they reproved her, reminding her that no one is necessary anywhere; the gap would be well taken care of, they knew. And then they sang a hymn.

Then through the hymn came another sound like the pain of a million broken hearts wrung out in one full drop, one sob. And a horror of great darkness was upon me, for I knew what it was—the Cry of the Blood.

Then thundered a voice, the voice of the Lord. "And He said, 'What hast thou done? The voice of thy brother's blood crieth unto me from the ground'."

The tom-toms still beat heavily, the darkness still shuddered and shivered about me; I heard the yells of the devil-dancers and weird, wild shriek of the devil-possessed just outside the gate.

What does it matter, after all? It has gone on for years; it will go on for years. Why make such a fuss about it?

God forgive us! God arouse us! Shame us out of our callousness! Shame us out of our sin![130]

---

[130] From *Things as They Are* by Amy Carmichael of the Dohnavur Fellowship. Reprinted by Bethany Fellowship, Inc., Minneapolis, Minnesota.

Appendix C

Christianity's Cruise

In the 1950s, Clifford wrote a sermon titled "Christianity's Cruise," based on the text Proverbs 24:11–12.

Christianity's Cruise

(The worst Cruise ever)

If thou forbear to deliver them that are drawn unto death, and those that are ready to be slain;

If thou sayest, Behold, we knew it not; doth not he that pondereth the heart consider it? and he that keepeth thy soul, doth not he know it? and shall not he render to every man according to his works?

These versus gripped me early in my Christian experience. Note four things:

1. **There are some in great peril.**

   "Those drawn onto death and those ready to be slain."

   The word peril implies physical danger, the serious or solemn prospect of death.

On Thursday, May 16, 1957 in the little town of Mansville on Long Island, just 70 miles from New York city, Mr. Hooper, a father of a small family was digging a dry shaft in his backyard to supplement his water supply. At 7:30 at night when the shaft was 24 feet down in sandy soil, Mr. Hooper dashed into the house for a pipe. Just then, his only son, 7 year-old Benjamin, came running into the yard with a playmate. He came to the 3 foot wide hole, and tried to jump over. He almost made it and for a second clung precariously on the edge. But the sand gave way beneath his feet and he slipped feet first into the well with his hands wedged above his head, his little red jacked pulled over his face. There he stayed entombed for 23 ½ hours almost completely covered by loose sand. Only his jacket near his mouth kept him from suffocation.

100 rescue workers poured in to help. A vertical shaft was dug 12 feet away then a horizontal tunnel until Benjamin was reached. 50 search lights played on the scene. There were ambulances—fire trucks—

oxygen equipment for a hose down near his mouth—doctors—nurses—neighbours—newspaper men—radio commentators—400 visitors.

A wonderful deliverance.

A wonderful rescue.

Do you know what I was thinking? If there is such a concern about someone in physical peril, what about those in spiritual danger? If there is so much effort to rescue a person in physical danger, why is it we do so little to deliver those who are in spiritual peril?

Every night a city larger than Saskatoon disappears. Yet, no news item in the paper. Every year a population as large as Great Britain is blotted out. Yet, in year-end summary of world events no mention is made of it.

When a man is executed (I saw in China 3 or 4 soldiers being shot) you cannot forget it but if our eyes were open to see as God sees we would behold not one human being but a great procession of men, women and children in great spiritual peril passing without hope into a Christless eternity.

2. **On the part of others there is a shameful neglect.**

Some are in danger.

Others know about that danger but shamefully neglect to do anything to deliver.

We can kill folks by just doing nothing. Did you know that?

David didn't slay Uriah but he did.

Ahab didn't slay Naboth but he did.

Mordecai said to Esther: If you do nothing we Jews will all perish.

"Think not with thyself that thou shalt escape in the king's house, more than all the Jews. For if thou altogether holdest thy peace at this time, then shall there enlargement and deliverance arise to the Jews from another place; but thou and thy father's house shall be destroyed."

Esther answered: "I will go into the king's presence and speak. If I perish, I perish"—but, I will do something.

Yes, there is an awful indifference and neglect to the needs and peril of a perishing world. Very little concern—real deep concern.

3. **There is no use to make excuses for ourselves.**

"If thou sayest, Behold, we knew it not."

This may be true—but the excuse is insufficient to deliver us from consequences. There is such a thing as corporate responsibility—communal responsibility. Take note of Deuteronomy 21:1–9. What was the community to do if they found a dead man? Notify police—as we do today?

Elders go out and measure to determine which city is closest to the body. The closest town or city was responsible. All the people of that place were responsible. Then the elders of that place would take a heifer, lead it down into an uncultivated valley and cut the head off. Afterwards, they would take a receptacle of water and all of them would wash their hands and all of them say "Our hands have not shed this blood, neither have our eyes seen it. Be merciful, O Lord, unto thy people Israel, whom thou hast redeemed, and lay not innocent blood unto thy people of Israel's charge."

Thus when they had slain the heifer in the valley and pleaded their innocence, and asked God for forgiveness—forgiveness and cleansing were granted on the basis of Christ's atoning work on Calvary (foreshadowed in the animal slain on that occasion).

What did it teach?

Communal responsibility.

"We don't know him—we know nothing about this murder—we had nothing to do with it."

You are responsible in a measure.

4. **A solemn responsibility.**

"Doth not He that pondereth the heart consider it?"

Do you know the real meaning of "pondereth?" It means "weighing." God is weighing us and testing us right now.

God gives every one of us a strange and awful freedom to do as we please—but there is a judgement ahead, yea it has begun already—even now.

We can go on doing what we like (no thunderbolt will strike us down). We can go on in life doing what we please (no flash of light will blind us). We can go on living in selfishness and ease—spending all our means on ourselves—but there is a reckoning.

It is taking place now—(present tense).

Our attitudes and actions are being weighed in God's scales. You remember Belshazzar and his drunken feast when he took the vessels of gold and silver which had been taken from the House of the Lord in Jerusalem and sacrilegiously used them for drink and praised his dead idols—but a living hand appeared near the wall of the palace and wrote on the wall before him,

"Thou art weighed in the balances and art found wanting."

The weighing had been going on while he was carrying on his godless sacrilegious orgy—and that night he was slain and the city was taken by the Medes and Persians.

Appendix D

God's Faithfulness

One example of God's faithfulness in meeting all Hudson's financial needs occurred when he was employed by a Dr. Hardey, who was often remiss in paying Hudson's salary.

> At Hull my kind employer . . . wished me to remind him whenever my salary became due. This I determined not to do directly, but to ask that God would bring the fact to his recollection, and thus encourage me by answering prayer.
>
> At one time, as the day drew near for the payment of a quarter's salary, I was as usual much in prayer about it. The time arrived but Dr. Hardey made no allusion to the matter. I continued praying. Days passed on and he did not remember, until at length on settling up my weekly accounts one Saturday night, I found myself possessed of only one remaining coin—a half-crown piece. Still, I had hitherto known no lack, and I continued praying.
>
> That Sunday was a very happy one. As usual my heart was full and brimming over with blessing. After attending divine service in the morning, my afternoons and evenings were taken up with Gospel work in the various lodging-houses I was accustomed to visit in the lowest part of the town. . . .
>
> After concluding my last service about ten o'clock that night, a poor man asked me to go and pray with his wife, saying that she was dying. I readily agreed, and on the way asked him why he had not sent for the priest, as his accent told me he was an Irishman. He had done so, he said, but the priest refused to come without a payment of eighteen pence, which the man did not possess as the family was starving. Immediately it occurred to my mind that all the money I had in the world was the solitary half-crown, and that it was in one coin; moreover, that while the basin of water-gruel I usually took for supper was awaiting me, and there was sufficient in the house for breakfast in the morning, I certainly had nothing for dinner on the coming day.
>
> Somehow or other there was at once a stoppage in the flow of joy in my heart. But instead of reproving myself I began to reprove the poor man, telling him that it was very wrong to have allowed matters to get

into such a state as he described, and that he ought to have applied to the relieving officer. His answer was that he had done so, and was told to come at eleven o'clock the next morning, but that he feared his wife might not live through the night.

"Ah," thought I, "if only I had two shillings and a sixpence instead of this half-crown, how gladly would I give these poor people a shilling!" But to part with the half-crown was far from my thoughts. I little dreamed that the truth of the matter simply was that I could trust God plus one-and-sixpence, but was not prepared to trust Him only, without any money at all in my pocket.

My conductor led me into a court, down which I followed him with some degree of nervousness. I had found myself there before and at my last visit had been roughly handled. . . . Up a miserable flight of stairs into a wretched room he led me, and oh, what a sight there presented itself! Four or five children stood about, their sunken cheeks and temples telling unmistakably the story of slow starvation, and lying on a wretched pallet was a poor, exhausted mother, with a tiny infant thirty-six hours old moaning rather than crying at her side.

"Ah!" thought I, "if I had two shillings and a sixpence, instead of half-a-crown, how gladly should they have one-and-sixpence of it." But still a wretched unbelief prevented me from obeying the impulse to relieve their distress at the cost of all I possessed.

It will scarcely seem strange that I was unable to say much to comfort these poor people. I needed comfort myself. I began to tell them, however, that they must not be cast down; that though their circumstances were very distressing there was a kind and loving Father in heaven. But something within me cried, "You hypocrite! telling these unconverted people about a kind and loving Father in heaven, and not prepared yourself to trust Him without half-a-crown."

I nearly choked. How gladly would I have compromised with conscience, if I had had a florin and a sixpence! I would have given the florin thankfully and kept the rest. But I was not yet prepared to trust in God alone, without the sixpence.

To talk was impossible under these circumstances, yet strange to say I thought I should have no difficulty in praying. Prayer was a delightful occupation in those days. Time thus spent never seemed wearisome and I knew no lack of words. I seemed to think that all I should have to do would be to kneel down and pray, and that relief would come to them and to myself together.

"You asked me to come and pray with your wife," I said to the man; "let us pray." And I knelt down.

But no sooner had I opened my lips with, "Our Father who art in heaven," than conscience said within, "Dare you mock God? Dare you kneel down and call Him 'Father' with that half-crown in your pocket?"

Such a time of conflict then came upon me as I had never experienced before. How I got through that form of prayer I know not, and whether the words uttered were connected or disconnected. But I arose from my knees in great distress of mind.

The poor father turned to me and said, "You see what a terrible state we are in, sir. If you can help us, for God's sake do!"

At that moment the word flashed into my mind, "Give to him that asketh of thee." And in the word of a King there is power.

I put my hand into my pocket and slowly drawing out the half-crown gave it to the man, telling him that it might seem a small matter for me to relieve them, seeing that I was comparatively well off, but that parting with that coin I was giving him my all; but that what I had been trying to tell them was indeed true, God really was a Father and might be trusted. And how the joy came back in full flood tide to my heart! I could say anything and feel it then, and the hindrance to blessing was gone—gone, I trust, forever.

Not only was the poor woman's life saved, but my life as I fully realized had been saved too. It might have been a wreck—would have been, probably, as a Christian life—had not grace at that time conquered and the striving of God's Spirit been obeyed.

I well remember that night as I went home to my lodgings how my heart was as light as my pocket. The dark, deserted streets resounded with a hymn of praise that I could not restrain. When I took my basin of gruel before retiring, I would not have exchanged it for a prince's feast. Reminding the Lord as I knelt at my bedside of His own Word, "He that giveth to the poor lendeth to the Lord," I asked Him not to let my loan be a long one, or I should have no dinner the next day. And with peace within and peace without, I spent a happy, restful night.

Next morning my plate of porridge remained for breakfast, and before it was finished the postman's knock was heard at the door. I was not in the habit of receiving letters on Monday, as my parents and most of my friends refrained from posting on Saturday, so that I was somewhat surprised when the landlady came in holding a letter or packet in her wet hand covered by her apron. I looked at the letter, but could not make out the handwriting. It was either a strange hand or a feigned one, and the postmark was blurred. Where it came from I could not tell. On opening the envelope I found nothing written within, but inside a sheet of blank paper was folded a pair of kid gloves from which, as I opened them in astonishment, half-a-sovereign fell to the ground.

"Praise the Lord," I exclaimed, "four hundred per cent for a twelve hours' investment! . . . If we are faithful to God in little things, we shall gain experience and strength that will be helpful to us in the more serious trials of life.

This remarkable and gracious deliverance was a great joy to me as well as a strong confirmation of faith. But of course ten shillings, however economically used, will not go very far, and it was none the less necessary to continue in prayer, asking that the larger supply which was still due might be remembered and paid. All my petitions, however, appeared to remain unanswered, and before a fortnight elapsed I found myself pretty much in the same position that I had occupied on the Sunday night already made so memorable. Meanwhile I continued pleading with God, more and more earnestly, that He would Himself remind Dr. Hardey that my salary was due.

Of course it was not want of money that distressed me. That could have been had at any time for the asking. The question uppermost in my mind was, "Can I go to China, or will my want of faith and power with God prove so serious an obstacle as to preclude my entering upon this much-prized service?"

As the week drew to a close I felt exceedingly embarrassed. There was not only myself to consider. On Saturday night a payment would be due to my Christian landlady, which I knew she could not well dispense with. Ought I not, for her sake, to speak about the matter of the salary? Yet to do so would be, to myself at any rate, the admission that I was not fitted to undertake a missionary enterprise. I gave nearly the whole of Thursday and Friday, all the time not occupied in my necessary employment, to earnest wrestling with God in prayer. But still on Saturday morning I was in the same position as before. And now my earnest cry was for guidance as to whether I should still continue to wait the Father's time. As far as I could judge, I received the assurance that to wait His time was best, and that God in some way or other would interpose on my behalf. So I waited, my heart being now at rest and the burden gone.

About five o'clock that Saturday afternoon, when Dr. Hardey had finished writing his prescriptions, his last circuit for the day being done, he threw himself back in his armchair as he was wont and began to speak of the things of God. He was a truly Christian man, and many seasons of happy fellowship we had together. I was busily watching at the time a pan in which a decoction was boiling that required a good deal of attention. It was indeed fortunate for me that it was so, for without any obvious connection with what had been going on, all at once he said:

"By the by, Taylor, is not your salary due again?"

My emotion may be imagined. I had to swallow two or three times before I could answer. With my eye fixed on the pan and my back to the doctor, I told him as quietly as I could that it was overdue some little time. How thankful I felt at that moment! God surely had heard my prayer and caused him in this time of my great need to remember the salary, without any word or suggestion from me.

"Oh, I am so sorry you did not remind me," he replied. "You know how busy I am. I wish I had thought of it a little sooner, for only this afternoon I sent all the money I had to the bank. Otherwise I would pay you at once."

It is impossible to describe the revulsion of feeling caused by this unexpected statement. I knew not what to do. Fortunately for me the pan boiled up and I had a good reason for rushing with it from the room. Glad indeed I was to keep out of sight until after Dr. Hardey had returned to his house, and most thankful that he had not perceived my emotion.

As soon as he was gone, I had to seek my little sanctum and pour out my heart before the Lord before calmness, and more than calmness, thankfulness and joy were restored. I felt that God had His own way and was not going to fail me. I had sought to know His will early in the day, and as far as I could judge had received guidance to wait patiently. And now God was going to work for me in some other way.

That evening was spent, as my Saturday evenings usually were, in reading the Word and preparing the subject on which I expected to speak in the various lodging-houses on the morrow. I waited perhaps a little longer than usual. At last about ten o'clock, there being no interruption of any kind, I put on my overcoat and was preparing to leave for home, rather thankful to know that by that time I should have to let myself in with the latchkey, as my landlady retired early. There was certainly no help for that night. But perhaps God would interpose for me by Monday, and I might be able to pay my landlady early in the week the money I would have given her before, had it been possible.

Just as I was about to turn down the gas, I heard the doctor's step in the garden that lay between the dwelling-house and surgery. He was laughing to himself heartily, as though greatly amused. Entering the surgery he asked for the ledger, and told me that, strange to say, one of his richest patients had just come to pay his doctor's bill. Was it not an odd thing to do! It never struck me that it might have any bearing on my own case, or I might have felt embarrassed. Looking at it simply from the position of an uninterested spectator, I also was highly amused that a man rolling in wealth should come after ten o'clock at night to pay a bill which he could any day have met by a check with the greatest ease. It appeared that, somehow or other, he could not rest with this on his mind, and had been constrained to come at that unusual hour to discharge his liability.

The account was duly receipted in the ledger and Dr. Hardey was about to leave, when suddenly he turned and handing me some of the banknotes just received, said to my surprise and thankfulness:

"By the by, Taylor, you might as well take these notes I have no change, but can give you the balance next week."

Again I was left my feelings undiscovered, to go back to my little closet and praise the Lord with a joyful heart . . .[131]

---

[131] Taylor (1932), pp. 32–42.

Appendix E

Japanese Atrocities

Little is known and much less has been written about the atrocities committed by the Japanese military during their eight-year war against China. In 1931, when the Japanese Army invaded Manchuria, they set up a number of facilities for bacterial and chemical research. Their objectives were twofold: prevention of disease in the Japanese military, and the development of bacterial and chemical weapons of war. Most of the research involved experiments on live human beings, with test subjects that included Chinese civilians, criminals, and Allied prisoners of war transported from the Philippines. The sex or age of the subject did not matter; tests were conducted on men, women, children, and infants.

This disregard for human life and the cruelty of the experiments is a testament to the depravity of mankind, which, in this case, was channelled through the Japanese belief that they were a superior race. For centuries, the home islands of Japan had been geographically and culturally isolated from the rest of the world. This isolation led to an extreme sense of nationalism and superiority. Racially the Japanese were remarkably homogeneous with traditional cultural viewpoints and values. According to Shinto belief, the Emperor of Japan was a direct descendant of the goddess who had created the Japanese people and thus was considered a living god himself. Even the Tokyo War Crimes Tribunal[132] made mention of prewar Japanese racism, noting that, "The mind of the Japanese people was systematically poisoned with harmful ideas of the alleged racial superiority of Japan over other peoples of Asia and even the whole world."[133]

Japanese society was also steeped in Confucian thought, with a hierarchical respect for one's superiors and unwavering obedience to authority. Obedience was touted as a supreme virtue; individual self-worth was unimportant. A person's only value was derived from being a citizen of Japan, with unconditional loyalty to the emperor. As one Japanese soldier said, "The

---

[132] The Tokyo War Crimes Tribunal was a composite of Allied judges tasked with trying the political and military leaders of Japan for war crimes committed during WWII.
[133] Harris, p. 72.

highest honor a soldier could achieve during war was to come back dead: to die for the emperor was the greatest glory, to be caught by the enemy the greatest shame."[134]

By the 1930s, the Japanese educational system had become regimented and highly nationalistic. Discipline and order were of paramount importance, and abuse was used to establish and maintain it.

> It was common-place for teachers to behave like sadistic drill sergeants, slapping children across the cheeks, hitting them with their fists, or bludgeoning them with bamboo or wooden swords. Students were forced to hold heavy objects, sit on their knees, stand barefoot in the snow, or run around the playground until they collapsed from exhaustion. There were certainly few visits to the schools by indignant or even concerned parents.[135]

Even school subjects, particularly history, language arts, and science, were imbued with ideals of obedience and distorted to project an image of the Japanese people as a superior race.

An individual entering the military was already programmed to this way of thinking. This was further honed by the harshness and abuse of military training. Recruits were routinely hit with fists, beaten with buckled belts or heavy wooden rods, and kicked with army boots with studs in the sole. Some died under the brutal conditions and some committed suicide. As one recruit said,

> Every day, without fail, we would get hit. And that's where the spirit of obedience is born. It's like training a dog. Humans and animals are the same. If you hit them, they learn to obey.[136]

Besides the physical brutality, there was psychological abuse as well, achieved by assigning various humiliating and degrading tasks, such as having to wash their officer's dirty underwear. Recruits were also systematically trained to behave in a violent and savage manner. They were required to watch and practice actual beheadings and the bayoneting of others, as a means of desensitizing them to the aggressiveness expected of them in war. As one

---

[134] Chang, p. 58.
[135] Chang, p. 31.
[136] Gold, p. 224.

young soldier stated, "There was a concept in our education that one does not become an adult until he has killed someone."[137]

When serving in an occupied country, the Japanese soldier's aggressiveness was allowed full reign, further aided by his sense of superiority.

> It has often been suggested that those with the least power are often the most sadistic if given the power of life and death over people even lower on the pecking order, and the rage engendered by this rigid pecking order was suddenly given an outlet when Japanese soldiers went abroad. In foreign lands or colonized territories, the Japanese soldiers— representatives of the emperor—enjoyed tremendous power among the subjects. In China even the lowliest Japanese private was considered superior to the most powerful and distinguished native . . . The Japanese soldier had endured in silence whatever his superiors had chosen to deal out to him, and now the Chinese had to take whatever he chose to deal out to them.[138]

For whatever reason, the Japanese had virulent contempt for the Chinese people, frequently referring to them as pigs. One soldier even commented, "a pig is more valuable now than the life of a (Chinese). . . . That's because the pig is edible."[139] This contempt had been cultivated by decades of social and educational indoctrination.

Of all the human experiment laboratories established by the Japanese in Manchuria, Unit 731 was the most notorious. Situated thirteen miles from the city of Harbin, it employed 3,607 scientific and technical personnel. Like the other units, it had the best equipment and an abundance of funding provided by the Tokyo War Ministry, as well as profits from Japan's lucrative opium trade in Manchuria.

Unit 731 was specifically constructed for human experimentation and contained research laboratories, dissection rooms and cells for "patients." It was heavily guarded and its very existence, and most certainly its activities, was shrouded in secrecy. No visitors were allowed. Even the conscripted Chinese workmen who built the facility were executed when it was finished.

Japan had been interested in chemical warfare for some time. In the late 1920s the Japanese Army started producing poisonous gas on the small island

---

137 Gold, p. 224.
138 Chang, p. 217–218.
139 Chang, p. 218.

of Okunoshima, just a few minutes by boat from the port city of Hiroshima. Production focused on yperite, lewisite, cyanogen, and mustard gas. The work was highly secretive—so much so that the island's very existence was not recorded on Japanese maps.

Then in the 1930s, there was an attempt by the Japanese government to procure the yellow fever virus from the Rockefeller Institute in New York. Supposedly, the virus was to be used in the development of a vaccine. The request was made along with the official paperwork by a young doctor, Naito Ryiochi, from the Japanese Embassy in Washington. The request was denied. Then a Rockefeller technician was offered a $3,000 bribe for the virus. This approach also failed. Finally, in August 1939 a world-renowned Japanese bacteriologist, Dr. Miyagawa Yonetsugi, approached the laboratory director, Dr. Wilbur Sawyer, and asked for a supply of the virus. As with the other attempts, Dr. Sawyer refused.

In China, Japanese research focused on three principal contagions—anthrax, glanders, and bubonic plague, although numerous other pathogens were also investigated.[140] Once cultivated, whatever viruses or bacteria was being studied would be injected into the victim or "maruta,"[141] which was the term used for research subjects. As the disease spread throughout the person's body, the symptoms would be carefully tracked and documented. If the subject succumbed to their ordeal or if they were of no further research value, they would be killed and the body dissected to determine the progress of the disease on the internal organs. As one unit employee, Mitamo Kazuo, stated, the maruta were killed "because no more experiments could be performed on them in view of their exhausted state and unsuitability for further experimentation."[142] Sometimes the subjects were dissected while still alive. Such research was considered important and of significant value given that "the effects of infection cannot be obtained accurately once the person dies because putrefactive bacteria set in,"[143] and could contaminate the findings. So, if a functioning human brain was required, a guard would

---

[140] Research also focused on cholera, typhoid, dysentery, tetanus, tuberculosis, typhus, gas gangrene, smallpox, diphtheria, pneumonia, meningitis, venereal disease, scarlet fever, whooping cough, salmonella, and botulism.
[141] Maruta is translated "log" in Japanese.
[142] Chan, p. 35.
[143] Gold, p. 44.

smash the victim's head open with an axe, extract the brain, and then rush it to the laboratory for immediate examination.

Descriptions of the vivisections were often provided with the most vivid and lurid detail. One young member of the Army Youth Corps reported that some maruta "were tied down and cut open while fully conscious. At first the maruta would let out a hideous scream, but soon the voice would stop." The same member talked about making "a long cut from the neck down" to slice the body open, remarking, "It's simple—anyone can do it."[144] Surprisingly, the man had significant qualms about disinterring and dissecting the bodies of people who had died from the plague, stating, "that was the most distasteful job I had: violating people's graves."[145] Other descriptions noted that "even with the intestines and organs exposed, a person does not die immediately. . . . The researchers then conduct their examination of the organs, remove the ones they want for study, then discard what is left of the body. Somewhere in the process, the victim dies through blood loss or removal of vital organs."[146]

Sometimes experiments were conducted simply out of curiosity or for the refinement of methods of torture, as opposed to the furtherance of scientific knowledge. These included such experiments as hanging a person upside down to determine the speed at which it took to choke to death, injecting air into a victim to test how fast an embolism would develop, or electrocuting victims at various voltages—sometimes upwards of 20,000 volts—to determine their lethality and effect on the body.

Words cannot express the horror and despicable nature of these experiments, even when they were conducted to better understand a disease's process in order to combat it more effectively. Dr. Kitano Masiji's work on tick encephalitis was one such research project. It involved injecting a mouse brain suspension into a victim. After a period of seven to ten days, symptoms would appear that were common in all cases. In curt research language, the scientist noted that, "Fever is the first change. When the fever begins to subside, motor paralysis appears in the upper extremities, neck, face, eyelids, and respiratory muscles. There are no significant sensor changes. No paralysis

---

[144] Gold, p. 170.
[145] Gold, p. 172.
[146] Gold, pp. 44–45.

is observed in the tongue, muscles of deglutition, or lower extremities. After recovery, paralysis may be permanent."[147]

Of all their research endeavours, Japanese scientists' primary focus was in developing pathogens and determining their most effective means of distribution. To be a viable weapon, a bacteria or virus needed to have certain properties. It needed the ability to be cultivated quickly and in mass quantities, and to maintain its vitality for a long period of time. It also needed to be sufficiently powerful to infect immediately, to be contracted speedily by others and be fatal, and to be disseminated easily. Because of their low cost and efficiency in killing large numbers of people, they were considered to be an effective weapon of war.

One method used to disseminate pathogens was through human contact. In this scenario, Chinese civilians would be captured and infected with the disease, then released back into their home community. Later the scientists would return and analyze the spread of the disease. Certain foods, fabrics, and metals were tested as possible germ carriers. Because produce was found to be a viable conduit, viruses were injected into various fruits, vegetables, and pastries. One member of Unit 731 recounted that one

> ... method involved placing the pathogens into buns and then wrapping them in paper. The Unit 731 men went to an area of the city where children were playing, and started eating buns similar to those in which they had planted the germs. The children saw the men eating, and came over. Then, the men gave the children the infected buns.[148]

Dogs were also used as a means of dissemination. In one experiment, dogs from a small village were rounded up, fed pork laced with cholera germs, then released.

> When the disease finished incubating and became active, the dogs would vomit. Then other dogs would come along and eat the vomit, and they, too, would become infected. The dogs would also be stricken with diarrhea and the feces would spread the disease among other dogs and to people. Some twenty percent of those who contracted the illness died.

---

[147] Harris, p. 85.
[148] Gold, pp. 229–30.

Survivors told of hearing the cries of sick people from their homes as they suffered.[149]

Later, cholera was found to be a very poor choice as a weapon given its incubation period of twenty days, whereas the plague had an incubation period of only three days.

Other animals were used as germ carriers including horses, pigs, and rats. Once infected, they would be released into various communities to spread the disease. Plague carrying fleas were also released.

Contamination of water supplies proved a good form of dissemination, whereby typhoid, glanders, and plague bacteria were introduced into rivers and wells. Then when a community was infected, the army would attack, forcing villagers to flee to other places and subsequently spread the disease. Crops were also infected. Japanese researchers would infect wheat and watermelon seeds with typhoid and cholera and then cultivate them to determine how much of the disease was retained in the plant. Sometimes soil and grass surfaces were infected with anthrax. The means of dissemination were endless, limited only by the boundaries of Japanese imagination. And the purpose of it all was to reduce the fighting power of the Chinese people, the axiom being that a disease-ridden and starving people significantly reduced in numbers is not an effective opponent. Another purpose was to exterminate as much of the population as possible.

Besides pathogens, various chemicals and gases were investigated as possible weapons of war, and again, humans were used as the testing materials. One method of experiment was to place several maruta wearing electronic monitoring equipment in a large chamber. Then liquefied phosgene gas would be released into the chamber. As the gas spread and asphyxiated the victims, their vital signs were recorded until death occurred. Afterward the bodies would be dissected to determine organ damage.

Researchers were interested in determining the lethality and disabling effects of different gases including mustard gas, lewisite, cyanic acid gas, phosgene gas, gas gangrene, carbon monoxide, hydrogen, and cyanide. Methods of dispensing the gases varied. Some were distributed using pipe bombs, chemical grenades, and mortar or heavy artillery shells of various

---

[149] Gold, p. 70.

calibrations. Others were released from airplanes flying at low altitudes. Pathogens also were distributed in this manner.

Further human experiments were conducted in order to quickly train new doctors in treating casualties on the battlefield. Vivisections and amputations were performed on healthy captives, to provide experience for new doctors. Practice in the removal of bullets was acquired by shooting a victim in the stomach; anaesthesia was never used. For hypodermic practice, air would be injected into a victim's veins. After the war, one Japanese medical personnel, Yuasa Ken, commented, "I operated on living Chinese for whom I had no hatred whatsoever to gain surgical ability in order to win the war."[150]

Research was also needed to develop vaccines, to keep the Japanese forces healthy and in good fighting form. This type of research involved infecting a victim with the disease being studied, and then testing various methods of treatment. Other research involved inoculating a person against a particular disease and then infecting them with the disease to determine a vaccine's effectiveness.

Because of the high rate of syphilis among the enlisted men, it became a research priority. By learning how the disease developed, the military hoped to find a way of protecting their soldiers from contracting sexually transmitted diseases and, if already infected, how best to treat them. Typical experiments involved forcing a man to have sexual intercourse with an infected woman. Once the man was infected, the progress of the disease would be observed over a period of time. Live dissections would occur to determine the effect on internal organs at different stages of infection.

Because the Japanese military was expecting to fight the Russians at some point in WWII, they were concerned about frostbite and cold weather combat. When Japan occupied Manchuria, their soldiers suffered severe frostbite, which in many cases necessitated the amputation of fingers and toes; in Siberia, the weather conditions would be worse.

In the frostbite experiments, a victim's limbs, usually the arms and hands or legs and feet, would be exposed to below freezing temperatures or placed in an apparatus where the temperature could be varied, sometimes as low as -70°C. During the process, the limb would be struck regularly with a club to ensure it was adequately frozen. Sometimes the limb would shatter in the

---

[150] Gold, p. 207.

process. When the limb was completely frozen, it would make a sound like a wooden board being struck. Then the limb would be immersed in water of various temperatures to determine the best temperature to thaw human flesh with the least amount of tissue damage. This was determined to be 37°C. During the thawing process, the flesh and muscle would fall from the bones. The end result was always the same—gangrene and the rotting away of extremities. Infants of three months old or even younger were also exposed to these experiments.

Among the Chinese civilian population, the actual death toll from these experiments and unlawful weapons of war will likely never be fully known, although the numbers are expected to be exceedingly high. Tens of thousands of people killed in the most barbaric and torturous manner would be a low estimate. Ironsides wrote in his introduction to *While China Bleeds*, "The savagery of the Japanese beggars all power of description."

When Japanese authorities realized the war would be lost, they set out to destroy any evidence of these research units. All documentation and equipment that could not be carried away or had not already been sent to Japan were destroyed. Even some of the buildings were obliterated with explosives. Vast quantities of chemicals and toxic materials were dumped into rivers, some of which remained polluted even after fifty years. All employees were ordered never to speak of the units, and some were even provided with cyanide in case they were captured by Russian or American soldiers while fleeing Manchuria. After their return to Japan, the scientists were given large remunerations or substantive pensions for their work.

Although the Chinese government initially had raised the alarm about Japanese bacterial and chemical attacks—shortly after Manchuria was taken and throughout WWII—the world paid little attention. It was not until the Americans occupied Japan and were preparing for the War Crimes Trial that the issue was taken seriously. Anonymous letters started to arrive with accusations of human experimentation, and additional information was obtained from the scientists and researchers themselves. The employment of bacteriological weapons was a direct violation of the Geneva Protocol of 1925, which prohibited "the use in war of asphyxiating poisonous or other gases and of bacteriological methods of warfare."[151]

---

[151] Chan, p. 37.

Although American authorities were alarmed by the extensive research conducted by the Japanese, they were anxious to obtain the results, as research on chemical weapons was also being done at Fort Detrick in the United States. A deal was made—Japanese scientists were promised immunity from prosecution for war crimes in exchange for their research data. American officials also decided to keep the fact of such research secret, hidden from the American public and other countries like the USSR, with whom relations were becoming increasingly strained.

Interestingly enough, at the close of WWII, German medical doctors and scientists were being charged with war crimes and put on trial for human experimentation, whereas the Japanese scientists were being protected. The justification for this hypocrisy was that the complaints were primarily anonymous and the "alleged victims" were of "unknown identity," which meant the accusations could not be verified. Other complaints, like those from the Japanese Communist Party, were not considered credible. Then, there was the justification that even if the bacteriological weapon development was true, there was no evidence it was to be used in warfare.[152] Instead of being held accountable for their actions, the scientists were protected by American officials and rewarded in Japanese society. After the war, most of them obtained lucrative and esteemed jobs: some as presidents or professors at prestigious medical universities or associations; as managers of various government departments; and as directors of large pharmaceutical companies or medical research laboratories. One physiologist, Dr. Yoshimura, who had directed the frostbite experiments in Manchuria, became an eminent authority on polar human biology.

The interest and importance of the Japanese research for the United States outweighed the disgust at and lack of morality in how it was obtained. Dr. Edwin Hill, Chief of Basic Sciences at Fort Detrick, Maryland, wrote that the data gathered by enemy scientists was secured "at the expenditure of many millions of dollars and years of work. . . . Such information could not be obtained in our own laboratories because of scruples attached to human experimentation."[153] Lieutenant Col. Robert McQuail, a member of US Army Intelligence, was well aware of the human experiments and the injection of bubonic plague bacilli in captured American soldiers, yet he commented matter-of-factly: "Naturally, the results of these experiments are of the highest intelligence value."[154]

---

[154] Harris, p. 259.

Appendix F

John Birch

May 28, 1918–August 25, 1945

John Birch was a Baptist missionary serving in China. Later, during WWII, when the United States was aligned with China in their fight against Japan, John was employed by the American Armed Forces as an intelligence officer. Although John was an American citizen, he was actually born in Landour, India, where his parents worked as missionary educators at Ewing Christian College. In 1920, the family returned to the United States and settled in Georgia, where John was raised and received his seminary training.

In July of 1940, John set sail for China; he was twenty-two years of age. After learning the language, he settled in Hangchow. But when Japanese forces overran the city, he moved south to Shangjao, in Free China. Had John remained in Hangchow he would have been imprisoned by the Japanese Army alongside other American nationals. It was in Shangjao where he became acquainted with Clifford.

On one of his travels in the area, John encountered Doolittle and several of his men. After crash landing in China, Doolittle was attempting to make his way overland to Chungking, the wartime capital of China. John was able to help him, acting as his interpreter and securing safe passage through the countryside; Doolittle was impressed with his abilities. Not only was John fluent in Chinese but also he showed exceptional diplomatic skills in obtaining Chinese military and civilian cooperation, and later in coordinating the evacuation of the airmen back to the United States.

By then, John had wanted to help with the war effort, so he applied to be a chaplain with the United States forces in China but was turned down. Apparently the seminary he attended was not accredited and he was not an ordained minister. Despite the setback, he was offered an intelligence position under General Chennault's Air Force command. On July 4, 1942, John officially commenced his military duties but was still allowed to carry on some of his missionary activities. Whenever possible, he held church services for the American servicemen, preached to the Chinese military and civilian populations, and substituted for the Army chaplains.

As an intelligence officer, John's work was clandestine and often conducted at great peril to himself. One of his assignments was to set up surveillance networks behind Japanese lines and train local Chinese citizens to operate the radio equipment. These networks obtained vital information on the location and strength of Japanese forces and relayed this information to Chennault's pilots. The pilots then bombed the designated targets. As a result, numerous battalions of Japanese soldiers and supply depots, as well as cargo and naval ships along the coast and Yangtze River were destroyed. John also operated on the front lines, supplying intelligence to Chinese generals, coordinating air strikes with Chinese ground forces, and arranging supply drops. He corrected aerial maps based on his travels through the country and secured medical supplies for hospitals.

John's work was endless and the enemy ever-present and relentless. By the early 1940s, there were 3 million Japanese in China, half of whom were in the armed forces, with the Japanese controlling most of the country north of the Yangtze River.

John continued with his intelligence activities. He coordinated the construction of several airfields, some adjacent to Japanese-held territory and others behind Japanese lines. The airfields were used to provide supplies to forward Chinese fighting units and refuel American planes for extended aerial combat missions. With the refuelling stations, Chennault's planes were able to leave base and bomb a designated target, then refuel at the airstrip and re-bomb the same area on their return to base.

John also coordinated rescue missions for downed American pilots behind Japanese lines. He arranged to have the captured airmen brought to the airfields by sympathetic Chinese citizens, where they were picked up and flown to safety. Over a span of two years, 1943 and 1944, John was able to save more than fifty American pilots. Missionaries were also rescued in this way, having become another prime target of Japanese persecution.

The Chinese people were an integral part of these rescue missions, as well as being responsible for maintaining the airfields. In summer, they repaired the runways; in winter, they removed any fallen snow. One time, when one of the airstrips was covered in fourteen inches of snow, eight hundred local citizens—men, women, and children—literally carried the snow from the field using hand shovels and buckets in a matter of hours.

When involved in a covert mission, John would disguise himself as a coolie, even to the extent of carrying a load suspended from a bamboo pole across his shoulders. He would dye his hair black and wear peasant clothes—a blue cotton jacket and trousers, and straw sandals. Because he presented as Chinese both in appearance and language, he was able to move about freely and even stop and talk with the Japanese soldiers without suspicion.

Ten days after WWII ended, John was murdered by communist soldiers. He had been on his way to Suchow in northeast China to officially arrange for the surrender of the city and to take charge of a nearby airfield. It was supposed to be his last mission before he returned to the United States. Accompanying him were three other American officers, as well as Lt. Tung of the Chinese Nationalist Army and several other men who spoke Japanese and were to act as interpreters. John was the commanding officer.

Nearing the end of his trip, John's party came across a group of communist soldiers ripping up railway tracks and taking down telegraph poles and wires. When the war ended with Japan on August 15, 1945, the Communist Army was focused on taking control of previously held Japanese territory. By disrupting communications and travel, and taking command of the airfields, they hoped to prevent the Nationalist Army from entering the area. Although Japanese garrisons in the vicinity were friendly and cooperative, the communist soldiers proved to be antagonistic and ruthless. In a nearby Chinese village, communist soldiers had killed most of the men, desecrated the local church, and confiscated all the village medical supplies.

Travelling on, John and his small party arrived at the outskirts of Hwang Kao, where they were detained by communist troops. John and Lt. Tung went in search of the officer-in-charge, while the rest of the men remained with the luggage and equipment. Eventually John was able to locate someone who appeared to be in charge but wouldn't identify himself as such. The man ordered his soldiers to take John's sidearm, but before they could do so, the man gave a second order to shoot both men. Two shots rang out. The first hit Lt. Tung in the right leg, a few inches above the knee; the second hit John in the upper left thigh. The bullets used by the communists were known as dumdum bullets, which had been outlawed under the Hague Rules of War in 1907. Because the bullets expanded on impact, they created large wounds that were exceedingly painful and quickly incapacitated the victim.

After Lt. Tung was shot, several soldiers smashed in his head with their rifle butts. Meanwhile, John's feet were bound and his hands tied behind his back. He was forced to kneel and then shot in the back of the head. Afterwards, the soldiers slashed his face repeatedly with their bayonets, grotesquely mutilating any recognizable features and making identification impossible. Later, the bodies of the two men were dragged to an open pit at the edge of the village. There, the bodies lay from mid-afternoon to evening, when an elderly woman chanced by. She was worried that the men's spirits would haunt the village at night if left in the open air. When the villagers went to move the bodies, they discovered that Lt. Tung was still alive. He was taken to a shelter and given whatever medical attention was possible. John was dead and was buried nearby.

The remaining men from John's group, who had stayed behind with the equipment, were captured and forced to march to Yenan, the communist stronghold in Shensi. The journey took two months. Sometime later, and only after General Wedemeyer, Commander of the US forces in China, made a personal appeal to Mao Tse-tung, were the men released.

On August 29, Lt. Miller, a colleague of John's, arrived in Suchow expecting to meet him there. Upon arrival, he heard about the murder of an American army captain and, learning that the captain's Chinese name was Pai Shang-wei, he surmised it was John. By then Lt. Tung had been transported to the hospital in Suchow, where he had his leg amputated and one eye removed as a result of the attack. After speaking with Lt. Tung, Miller went to the morgue to view John's body, which had been disinterred by the Nationalist Army. Because of the mutilation, the only way to identify John was by a missing bridge in his teeth and his body build.

Lt. Miller and General Mori, the Japanese Commander of Suchow who had been waiting to surrender the city to a government representative, arranged John's funeral. Two American pilots who had died when they crash-landed at the Suchow airport were to be buried with him.

At the appointed hour the entire Japanese high command in Suchow, twenty high-ranking officers, Chinese officials and other leading citizens marched solemnly with Lieutenant Miller into the towering Catholic cathedral for a requiem high mass.

Following the mass, a mournful Japanese military band led a procession through the streets of the city. Twenty-four Chinese coolies carried the flag-draped coffin to the burial site on a wooded slope of the Hung-lung Mountain overlooking the south side of Suchow.

The three American officers were to be interred in side-by-side crypts, with John in the center. At the graveside a Chinese Protestant minister performed the final rites, followed by Latin prayers from the priests. As the coffins were eased into their final resting places, a Japanese drummer beat a sad farewell while the crowd of dignitaries, Confucianists, Buddhists, Shintoists, Catholics and a few Protestants stood in respectful silence. Then at the command of a Japanese officer, three rifle salutes were sounded and the masons began cementing the stones in place. After the crypts were secured, the workmen stencilled vital statistics at the front of each vault . . .[155]

Under John's name and the date of his death were the words, "He died for the cause of righteousness." He was twenty-seven years of age.

The US War Department attempted to cover up the fact that John was murdered. His war record was classified as "secret," and it was reported that he had been struck by a stray bullet which killed him instantly. No mention was made of him having been deliberately killed by communist soldiers, despite the facts being well known throughout China. News agencies were also silenced, for fear of further jeopardizing the already unstable relations with the Communist Party. And when John's personal effects were sent to his parents, his diary was missing. Although John probably documented his missions, most likely in obscure terms, it is possible that the diary also contained his observations of communist duplicity. Some anti-communist groups believed that John was deliberately killed to prevent him from disseminating unfavourable information about the communists as he was quite vocal on the subject.

During his three years with the army, John was critical of the communists, whereas U.S. State Department officials presented Mao as simply an agrarian

---

155 Hefley, pp. 187–188.

democratic reformer, and supported him and the Communist Party over the legitimate government of China. General Stilwell, who had preceded General Wedemeyer as Commander of the U.S. Armed Forces in China, also championed the communists. John's experience taught him otherwise. From John's forays and contact with communist guerillas, he knew the communists were not reformers and were not interested in fighting the Japanese as it would deplete their own numbers. Other nonpartisan and missionary reports provided similar opinions and documented accounts of communist malfeasance.

On one foray behind enemy lines, John's radio network informed him of the location of a large contingent of Japanese troops, including a supply train with over a hundred cars loaded with armoured vehicles, howitzers, and other war equipment. John was aware that communist guerillas were active along the railway but had not interfered with the troop movement or even informed anyone of the Japanese presence. Combined with other similar incidents, John surmised the communists were reserving their resources, hoping the Japanese Army would deplete the nationalist forces, so it would be easier for them to take over China when the time came.

Additional support for John's beliefs was provided when the communists sabotaged the dikes on the Yellow River. When the dikes were breached, floodwaters inundated the crops in the nationalist-held province of Anhwei, causing a shortage of food and bogging down nationalist troops.

Ironically, when Chiang Kai-shek was fighting the communists before and during the earlier part of the Sino-Japanese War, the communists used the slogan "Chinese should not fight Chinese" to turn the focus from themselves as the enemy. Yet when WWII ended and Japan surrendered, they had no problem slaughtering millions of Chinese in their conquest for control of the country.

John saw communism as an evil force in the world. He predicted that after the war, the communists would try to overthrow the government and then make a move on Korea in their quest for world domination. Although communism was touted as a "party of the people for the people," it also maintained that the masses were not sufficiently ready or educated enough to rule themselves, so they must be guided and led by men who had the knowledge to do so. In all practicality, China became a communist dictatorship, the same as in Russia.

The Chinese communists never apologized for John's death and only reluctantly acknowledged it. Instead, they provided various excuses for why it happened. One excuse was that the soldiers thought John was a Japanese disguised as an American serviceman.

In response to the threat of communism, an American, Robert Welch, organized an anti-communist society in 1958, which he named in John's honour—the John Birch Society.

Appendix G

Fate of Captured Doolittle Raiders

Within several days of the deaths of Dieter and Fitzmaurice, the three surviving members of crew number six were captured by the Japanese Army. On April 24, 1942, the men—Dean Hallmark, Robert Meder, and Chase Nielsen—were flown to Shanghai, where they were interrogated and tortured to obtain information about the raid on Japan. Japanese authorities were skeptical that heavy-weight bombers could actually disembark from the deck of an aircraft carrier.

The second crew to meet a similar fate was crew number sixteen, piloted by William Farrow. The other crew members included Robert Hite, George Barr, Harold Spatz, and Jacob DeShazer. Farrow's plane left the Navy carrier at 0920 hours. After successfully bombing an aircraft and an oil tank compound, the crew flew to China where they bailed out near Ningpo, in Japanese-held territory. There were no major injuries other than DeShazer fracturing several ribs when he landed on a grave mound. In less than twenty-four hours the crew was apprehended. Like Hallmark's crew, the men were interrogated and brutalized. They were beaten and kicked, refused sleep, and kept isolated from each other in solitary confinement. Barr became deaf in one ear from a blow to the head by a rifle butt.

Next came various forms of torture, one of which was water torture:

> The victim was bound or handcuffed with his hands behind him and forced to lie on his back on the floor. Guards would hold or sit on his legs. Another would sit on his stomach while another would pin the prisoner's head between his knees to keep his head facing upward. A towel was placed in cuplike fashion over the mouth and nose. A guard would then take a bucket of water and pour it into the towel until the victim lost consciousness. The result was literally like drowning and the Kempei Tai[156] experts knew exactly how far they could go and still bring a person back to life. They would let the victim loose and apply pressure to his lungs, sometimes by jumping on his abdomen, to force the water out. After the coughing and sputtering stopped, the process

---

[156] The Japanese Army's military police comparable to the Nazi Gestapo.

was repeated several more times until the victim grew so weak he lost all strength to resist the treatment. At this point, the torture would suddenly cease and the questioning resume.[157]

On May 22, each man was forced to sign a confession prewritten for them in Japanese. Afterwards they were placed together in one cell in a makeshift military prison. The cell was small and cramped, and none of the men were able to lie down to sleep. But the food was the worst part of their ordeal.

> Meals if they could be called that, were "served" three times a day. The menu consisted solely of yellowed watery rice and weak tea. The rice was obviously taken from the scrapings left after meals had been prepared for the prison staff. Served in chipped enamel pans, the yellow grains were mixed with pebbles, worms, maggots and dirt.[158]

Because of the starvation diet, the men's thoughts constantly turned to food. They thought about it, talked about it, and planned their favourite meal to eat when they were released home.

The men remained in the one cell, never leaving it for seventy days. They could not shave, wash, or remove their clothes. Their "bodies were covered with welts from the lice and bedbugs which infested the cell and nested in their clothes." Rats lived under the cell floor and would come out at night to nibble the grains of rice that had slipped into the cracks in the floor or on an occasional body part. The men took turns staying awake at night to fend them off.

Meanwhile, Japanese authorities were debating the men's fate. Army officials wanted the death penalty, but that required them to be charged as war criminals under the jurisdiction of a Japanese court. At that time there was no military law covering raids by enemy forces, so a new law had to be enacted and applied after the fact. The new law stated that any individual who had committed an act of bombing, strafing, or attacking civilians with the objective of cowing, intimidating, killing, or maiming them was liable for the death penalty. The irony of it all was that Japan had violated every aspect of their own law in every country they had attacked or occupied before and during WWII, and certainly in China.

---

[157] Glines (1966), pp. 75–76.
[158] Glines (1966), p. 94.

Despite the eight men's fate being sealed, a trial was set for them for August 28. All were found guilty of war crimes and all were sentenced to death. But just before their execution, the sentences of Meder, Nielsen, Barr, and DeShazer were commuted to life imprisonment.

October 15, 1942. In late afternoon on a foggy, overcast day, Hallmark, Farrow, and Spatz were driven out to an old Chinese cemetery where three small wooden crosses had been erected. Each man was ordered to kneel with his back to a short cross while his arms were tied to the crossbeam. Each man had a blindfold placed around his head with a spot of black ink dabbed on the cloth to mark the centre of his forehead. The firing squad raised their rifles and, when given the order, fired. Upon impact, each man's head snapped back and then slumped forward. Blood stained the blindfold and dripped to the ground below. It was over.

For most of their captivity, the remaining airmen were kept in solitary confinement. Realizing they needed to keep their minds stimulated, each man devised his own mental activity. Nielsen used his imagination to build a house. He started with the floor plan, dug the basement, put up the framework, and shingled the roof. Then he covered the framework brick by brick. Next came the interior decorating. He decided on colours and all the fixtures, and carefully painted and installed everything. Finally he did the landscaping. In turn, Hite planned out a model farm from the clearing of the land to the pounding in of the last fence post. DeShazer composed poetry on a mental blackboard and erased each poem before starting the next. Meder reviewed books he had read earlier in life, composed philosophical essays, and recited poetry.

Later the men asked for reading material. The only books that could be found for them in English were four Christian books and a Bible. The men, particularly DeShazer, memorized the passages and recited them over and over. The Bible proved to be a great source of solace and sustenance for the men and resulted in an improvement in their mental outlook and morale.

Twenty-five years after the raid on Japan, four of the men—Nielsen, Hite, Barr, and DeShazer—composed an article about the impact of the Bible on their lives. The article was titled "The Battle Shall Be Won." In part, it said,

> (We) began to recognize the true meaning of religion when we were
> given the Bible to read. We found in its ripped and faded pages a source

of courage, and faith we never realized existed. The verses we had memorized as children suddenly came alive and as vital to us as food. We put our trust in the God we had not accepted before and discovered that faith in His word would carry us through the greatest peril of our lives.[159]

In the early winter months of 1943, Meder developed a severe case of dysentery, which left him extremely weak and dehydrated. Then his legs started to swell—one of the first signs of beriberi.[160] On December 1, 1943, he died. He had not received any medical care, but the attendant's report falsely claimed that he had received timely and appropriate treatment.

In August 1945, when Japan was close to surrender, the American government set a plan in motion to rescue all Allied prisoners of war, fearing they would be executed before they could be liberated. Rescue teams were sent to various sites where POW camps were known to exist, including one near Peking. This is where the remaining Doolittle Raiders were being held. Had American intelligence not ascertained that some of the Raiders were still alive, it is likely that they would never have been released. Relief forces were also dispatched to Weihsien, where young Philip and the other missionary children were being held. When rescue teams arrived in China, they demanded the release of all prisoners. Although Japanese authorities stalled on whether they even had the Doolittle airmen, they eventually released them. The date was August 20, 1945. The men had been in solitary confinement for forty months and had survived brutal conditions, torture, and near starvation.

Just prior to release, Barr became seriously ill and slipped into unconsciousness. For eleven days he hovered between life and death, and when liberation came, he had to be carried from the prison on a stretcher. Nielsen, Hite, and DeShazer returned to the United States a few days later, but Barr had to remain behind because of his weakened condition. What followed was a nightmare of mental confusion, paranoia, and delusions. Barr was unable to grasp the reality of his freedom and believed that it was all a cruel trick by the Japanese. Then, when confined to a psychiatric unit with locked doors and barred windows, he became certain he was still in prison.

---

[159] Glines (1966), p. 219.
[160] A serious disease affecting the body's nerves. It affects a person's ability to concentrate, produces muscle and joint pain, and results in a loss of coordination and sense of well-being. It is common in parts of the world where polished rice is a staple diet.

On two occasions, he attempted suicide: first, by stabbing himself in the chest with a pocket knife; then by hanging using a lamp cord, though the cord broke under his weight. Even when he returned to the United States, he was confined to various mental health facilities for another two years. Only gradually did his emotional state improve.

Barr eventually obtained a master's degree in Physical Education and, after teaching for a year, became a management analyst for the US Army. Nielsen and Hite remained in the air force. After serving in the Korean War, Hite returned to civilian life and became a hotel manager while Nielsen later worked as a management engineer at an air force base in Utah. DeShazer became an ordained minister and returned to Japan as a missionary in the city of Nagoya, the very place he had bombed. At a reunion ceremony of the Raiders in 1950, all of the survivors voted to support DeShazer's missionary work.

Appendix H

Isobel Kuhn

Isobel Kuhn was a CIM missionary to the Lisu, a tribal people living in the mountainous region of Yunnan Province. The mountains, whose peaks reach as high as twelve to fifteen thousand feet, and the Salween Gorge, which runs through the area, comprise the border between China and Burma. To the east lies China, to the west Burma, and to the south the Burma Road. It was there that Isobel, her husband, John, and their young son Danny lived. Their oldest daughter Kathryn attended school at Chefoo and, like Philip, was interned by the Japanese at Weihsien.

By 1949 communist forces were entrenched in the area. They occupied the Mekong Valley and the Luda District in the east and north, and the Salween Canyon in the south. Although the Kuhns' little tribal village, which they called home, was six days' journey over the mountains from the nearest motor road, the communists were closing in. Then in December of that year, the governor of Yunnan unexpectedly surrendered the entire province to the communists. Isobel immediately recognized the danger her family was in. Communist officials could actually block them from leaving China, or imprison or even execute them. Furthermore, they could be caught in the fighting still being waged between the communists and the feudal lairds of the mountain villages. She and her young son had to flee. John had already been detained at Paoshan and would not be able to leave with them.

With most exits blocked by the communists, the only means of escape was through a narrow pass in the mountains. It would be a treacherous and formidable climb of eleven thousand feet, but it had to be attempted. On March 10, 1950, Isobel, six-year-old Danny, and several Lisu Christians set out from their small mountain village. Isobel rode a mule while Danny was carried in a mountain chair by two of the Lisu men. The first night they slept in a rice field by the side of the Salween River. By the third day, when they reached the lower slopes of the Pienma Mountain, they encountered rain, which meant that it would be snowing in the pass and that the trail along the top would be obliterated. To cross in such weather would have been extremely dangerous or even impossible. Every year travellers trying to cross in the snow perished. And if the snow remained, which it would at that time of year, the pass would be untravellable for several months. There was nothing they could do but turn back.

When faced with any obstacle, Isobel always resorted to seeking direction from God. Her standard prayer was, "Lord, if this obstacle is from you, I accept it; if it is from Satan, I refuse it."[161] And so, she set her mind to push onward, knowing that the Lord would either provide safe passage or hinder her way altogether.

On the sixth day of their journey, after several more days of rain, the small party started their final ascent. They left at 7:30 in the morning and climbed steadily—through the darkness and up through the clouds, which enveloped them like a fog. Around noon they encountered several Lisu men who had just crossed the pass. Apparently the snow was deep at the top—and it was still snowing—but if they hurried, they could follow the men's footprints. Although everyone was hungry and tired, it would have been fatal to delay for any reason. If the footprints became covered by the snow, the Kuhn's little party would have perished. At 6:00 p.m., having climbed for a continuous ten and a half hours, they reached the top of the pass. Isobel divided the only food she had with Danny—one piece of bread and a small portion of cheese.

In good weather, the trail at the top was no wider than a cow path. After winding back and forth on level ground for a short distance, it plunged suddenly down the side of the mountain. In the deep snow, the path was even more treacherous—and to make matters worse, a violent storm was brewing, with more snow coming down thick and heavy.

The going became so difficult that the two Lisu men found they could no longer carry Danny on the mountain chair, so one of them decided to carry him on his back. It was then that Danny began to sing "The Ninety and Nine"[162] at the top of his lungs.

> But none of the ransomed ever knew
> How deep were the waters cross'd;
> Nor how dark was the night that the Lord pass'd thro'
> Ere he found His sheep that was lost . . .

161Kuhn (1997), p. 196.
162A hymn written in 1868 by Elizabeth Clephane.

"Lord, whence are those blood-drops all the way,
That mark out the mountain's track?"

"They were shed for one who had gone astray
Ere the Shepherd could bring him back:"

"Lord, whence are thy hands so rent and torn?"

"They are pierced tonight by many a thorn . . ."

But all thro' the mountains thunder-riv'n,
And up from the rocky steep,
There arose a glad cry to the gate of heav'n,

"Rejoice! I have found My sheep!"
And the angels echoed around the throne,
"Rejoice! For the Lord brings back His own!"

Although Danny appeared quite comfortable throughout the storm, Isobel was drenched. The falling snow melted when it landed on her and drained into her rubber boots. Even with her feet immersed in ice cold snow water and the loss of feeling in her extremities, she pushed on.

As the party reached lower altitudes the snow turned to rain and the steep paths turned to mud. Isobel's mule had difficulty staying on its feet and started to slip dangerously. Isobel dismounted and proceeded on her own, slipping and sliding down the rest of the descent.

Finally they reached the valley below. They were in Burma, but not out of danger. Isobel had no visa, no Burmese money, and no guarantor to stand surety for her. Nor did she speak the language. She was worried upon presenting herself to the Burmese authorities that she would be detained or even returned to Communist China. She still had two more weeks of travel through the jungle, which was inhabited by wild elephants, tigers, and poisonous snakes. And there were more mountains to cross before they reached any semblance of civilization. Any fears she had were quickly discarded, believing that "the only fear a Christian should entertain is the fear of sin."[163]

After many more hardships and thousands of miles crossed, Isobel and Danny arrived safely in the United States, meanwhile John remained in China. Although detained by the communist government, he was eventually

---

[163] Kuhn (1997), p. 205.

"invited" to leave at the point of a bayonet. Denied exit through Burma, he was forced to trek across the whole of China to obtain passage to the United States. It was eighteen months before he was able to join Isobel.

Later, Isobel and John went as missionaries to the mountain tribes of northern Thailand. In 1954, Isobel was diagnosed with cancer. She died on March 20, 1957.

Appendix I

Arthur Mathews and Rupert Clarke

The CIM was the largest Protestant mission in China, and despite persecution by the communist government, all of its missionaries were able to leave their adopted country safely. The last to leave were Dr. Rupert Clarke and Arthur Mathews.

Dr. Clarke was a medical missionary in the small town of Hwalung in the Province of Tsinghai. Hwalung was situated near the Tibetan border, a place where Dr. Clarke was happy to be, as he had always wanted to work among the Tibetan people. When the communist persecution of foreigners began, Clarke was accused of murder because several of his patients had died after he had operated on them. Dr. Clarke was imprisoned and spent four days in a twelve-by-twelve cell with forty other prisoners. Twice a day they were fed a diet of coarse bread and water. After being released, he was confined to his compound and an old man was assigned to do his shopping.

When Dr. Clarke ran out of food and money, he considered taking food from the hospital storeroom. The hospital was part of the mission, so why not?

> He hesitated because he realized what would happen if the Communists discovered him taking it. In his mind's eye, he could see the headlines blazoned all over northwest China: "Mission doctor steals hospital food!" It was just the sort of incident that would make fine copy to bring the mission and all it stood for into disrepute.[164]

The matter was further decided when he recalled a verse in Proverbs, "Trust in the Lord with all thine heart; and lean not to thine own understanding."

In the same part of northwest China, Arthur Mathews and his family faced their own set of troubles. In 1950, Arthur accepted an invitation by a Chinese church in Hwangyuan to minister to the community there. Hwangyuan was close to Tibet and had a diverse population of Tibetans, Muslims, and Chinese civilians. Soon after their arrival, Arthur and his wife were informed by city officials that they could not do any mission work outside of their compound.

---

[164] Thompson, p. 151.

No preaching in the streets, giving out tracts, or dispensing medicine. And although they had expected to live in a large and spacious compound, they were confined to two small rooms. One was a little kitchen containing a large iron stove and a few basic pieces of furniture, while the other was a cramped bedroom on the second floor of the compound. The bedroom was unheated and icy cold, and to get to it, they had to go outside and up a flight of stairs.

After learning that their gospel work was to be seriously curtailed, Arthur applied for exit visas. For two months he waited, but the permits never came. Eventually, Arthur was summoned by a senior Chinese official who promised him the visas if he would spy for them. He refused, fully aware that the cost of his refusal could mean death. Every day large notices were posted on city walls with the names of people who were to be executed—those who did not cooperate with the new communist regime. Every day he heard the sounds of executions, and every day he saw new names added to the list.

Then came a request—he was asked to write a report on five of his fellow missionaries. Although Arthur did not know them personally, he wrote whatever glowing reports he had heard about them. Fortunately, before he could submit his report, a Chinese friend chanced by, saw what he had written, and stopped him. Apparently, a favourite tactic of the communists was to erase what was written, except for the signature at the bottom of the page, and insert their own condemnations.

Next came various accusations against Arthur, which stemmed from his previous post at Changyeh. These included such things as:

1. standing on a table belonging to the church
2. misusing a memorial plaque
3. killing a dog
4. locking the kitchen door at the church; and
5. closing the school at Changyeh.

Despite the ridiculousness of the charges, there was some substance of truth to them; he had killed a stray dog, but the deacon had asked him to kill it. Arthur pled guilty.

At that time, accusations were actively solicited by the Communist Party and, in fact, were required.

> Every single Chinese was forced to "criticize" himself and his neighbour in order to prove his loyalty to Communism—especially anyone who had had any connection with a foreigner. The Red Regime will not allow the belief that there can be any good American or Englishman. If you say so you are revealing the fact that you are pro-imperialist in your heart. You must accuse the foreigner . . . with some sin against the government in order to clear your own skirts of the suspicion that you are pro-imperialist. And to be pro-imperialist means death.[165]

Adapting to the new order of rule, Chinese Christians tended to denounce only those missionaries who had either died or were no longer living in the country. But, when that became unacceptable and they were required to speak out against missionaries actually living in their community, they typically mentioned only trivial or innocuous matters.

As time went on, new forms of persecution arose. First, the Mathews' money was frozen at the bank. The only way to obtain funds was to apply each month for whatever amount they needed. Once the chit was submitted, the amount had to be reviewed and Arthur would either have to wait or be told to come back another day. If he had to return, he would generally be given the same run around.

> More often than not (Arthur) was told to wait. Outside in all kinds of weather, snow, slush, rain as well as sunny skies, he had to hang around the entrance hour after hour, with the native passers-by staring at him. To laugh at the foreigner stood you in good stead with the government so there were those who would like to make fun of him. All this he must endure and at the end of the day be told to come back again.[166]

Invariably the amount granted was less than requested and certainly less than needed. Over time, the family was subsisting at a starvation level. Once, when down to pennies, which would only have bought them three match boxes—certainly no food or fuel—they had to wait six weeks for any money to come through official channels. But God saw their plight and provided sufficient funds for their needs—some arrived from the mission, through the postal service, and some from Chinese Christians, as well as gifts of food and clothing. One time they received a package of raisins, which Arthur's wife,

---

[165] Kuhn (1958), p. 75.
[166] Kuhn (1958), p. 62.

Wilda, doled out three at a time. In another instance, an old Tibetan woman, partially deaf and blind and so weak that she had to crawl up the steps to their door, presented them with six little cakes of steamed bread.

Still the communist persecution persisted. At various times, the Mathews were informed that their exit visas had been approved. Then when they had pared down their belongings, bought their bus tickets, and made their travel arrangements, they would be informed that they could not leave. Six times they were told they could leave and six times they were told they could not go. And each time they were left more destitute than before. Arthur and Wilda found this form of persecution the most trying, for when the promise of freedom is suddenly and inexplicably taken away, the human spirit breaks down.

The next step in their persecution was to place the family under house arrest, leaving them totally isolated. They were not allowed to leave their compound other than to go to the river to draw water or to the market to buy food. No one was allowed to talk to them or have anything to do with them. A spy was even placed in their compound to report any such breach to the authorities. They were not only destitute but completely enveloped by a shroud of silence.

As the winter of 1952 set in, their monies were so low that they could not afford to buy any coal for their stove, which was needed for heating, cooking, and the boiling of water. Like the poor of the land, Arthur was reduced to making coal balls by mixing coal dust with manure.

> And so he would select a seat out in the sun on those cold near-winter days and patiently mould coal dust and sheep dung with water from the river. For a gentleman to come in any contact with dirt, let alone manure, was unspeakably degrading in Chinese eyes. The melted snow-water made big cracks in his hands which were painful and yet he sat there day after day patiently moulding them. The Chinese who had to pass him were really touched. He heard one of them whisper, "Dear me, dear me! Look at this! Look at this!" But he smiled cheerfully and every evening together (he and Wilda) had a praise service to the Lord.[167]

At other times, when the Mathews had no money to buy milk for their three-year-old daughter Lilah, she did without. Neither the CIM nor its missionaries

---

[167] Kuhn (1958), pp. 80–81.

were to incur any debt or even buy on credit. If there was no money for something, it was not bought—not even food, not even when starving. God would provide.

And God was faithful and did provide, for Lilah never did go for long without milk. Once, when they were able to afford only a small amount of milk, they found it was much richer than before, and that it could be watered down to make it last longer. Another time, a young Christian man gave them money for milk saying he could live just as well eating only potatoes.

The Mathews' belief in God's faithfulness made a deep impression on the Chinese people. This lesson was particularly important for the Chinese church. With the expulsion of the missionaries from China, the church, a lingering example of Christian faith, became the primary target of communist persecution. Although the communist constitution upheld religious freedom, it also maintained the liberty to oppose religious faith.

Over two and a half years, the Mathews learned to accept God's will. They not only learned to accept and submit to it but also realized the importance of actually delighting in it. Even little Lilah was a testament to their faith and praise. One evening, while sitting down to a meagre meal of toasted bread, she began to sing:

> In heavenly love abiding,
> No change my heart shall fear;
> And safe is such confiding,
> For nothing changes here.
> The storm may roar without me,
> My heart may low be laid,
> But God is round about me,
> And can I be dismayed?[168]

Doubtless she had heard her parents singing the hymn and remembered the words.

On March 1, 1953, exit permits were finally granted, but only for Wilda and Lilah. Arthur was not allowed to go as there were new charges against him. The first charge was that he had collaborated in the murder of a Dr. Kao in 1936, even though Arthur was still living in the United States at the time.

---

[168] A hymn written by Anna L. Waring in 1850.

Four other charges followed: accusing a girl of being a communist, who was then tortured and "maimed for life" by nationalist forces; spreading sedition; being an imperialist; and seizing property not his own. Eventually Arthur was found guilty and sentenced to permanent deportation from China. Dr. Clarke was also on trial at the same time and received the same sentence. On June 20, 1953, both men crossed the makeshift wooden bridge that marked the border between China and Hong Kong. They were free!

Bibliography

Alm, Paul A. and Schmid, Byron L. *The Paulsons and Alms in America: The Family of Paul and Birthe Gilbertson.* 1991.

Austin, Alvyn J. *Saving China.* Toronto: University of Toronto Press, 1986.

Bosshardt, Alfred. *The Guiding Hand.* London: Hodder and Stoughton, 1973.

Brackman, Arnold C. *The Other Nuremberg: The Untold Story of the Tokyo War Crimes Trial.* New York: William Morrow and Company, Inc., 1987.

Brady, Anne-Marie. (Ed.). *A Foreign Missionary on the Long March: The Unpublished Memoirs of Arnolis Hayman of the China Inland Mission.* Portland, Maine: Merwinasia, 2011.

Burgess, Alan. *The Small Woman.* London: Pan Books Ltd., 1957.

Buruma, Ian. "Character Arc." *The New Yorker* (January 17, 2022): pp. 61–64.

Carmichael, Amy. *Thy Brother's Blood Crieth.* Minneapolis: Bethany Fellowship, Inc., (Unknown date).

Chan, Jenny. *The Khabarovsk War Crimes Trial.* U.S.A.: Pacific Atrocities Education, 2020.

Chang, Iris. *The Rape of Nanking.* U.S.A.: Basic Books, 1997.

Chang, Natasha. *Bound Feet & Western Dress.* New York: Bantam Books, 1997.

Chennault, Claire Lee. *Way of a Fighter.* New York: G. P. Putnam's Sons, 1949.

Clements, Ronald, and Metcalf, Steve. *In Japan the Crickets Cry.* Oxford: Monarch Books, 2010.

Cliff, Norman. *Courtyard of the Happy Way.* England: Arthur James Limited, 1977.

Cliff, Norman. (Ed.). *How Firm a Foundation*. Chefoo Schools Association, 2006.

Crossett, Margaret. *Harvest at the Front*. U.S.A.: China Inland Mission, 1946.

Doolittle, Gardner. *Wings of a Warrier*. Shelter Island, 2013. DVD.

Doolittle, James. *I Could Never Be So Lucky Again*. New York: Bantam Books, 1991.

Dowsett, Rose & Berry, Chad. (Ed.). *God's Faithfulness*. Singapore: Mainland Press Pte. Ltd., 2014.

Dreyer, Edith G. *Light and Shadow in China*. Philadelphia: Westbrook Publishing Company, 1949.

Dunn, Miriam. *My Children or the Cross*. Dalton, Ohio: P. Graham Dunn Publishing, 2011.

Fairbank, John. *China: A New History*. Cambridge, Massachusetts: The Belknap Harvard University Press, 1992.

Forester, C.S. *The Good Shepherd*. Great Britain: Hunt Barnard & Co. Limited, 1967.

Francis, Lesley. *Winds of Change in China*. Singapore: Overseas Missionary Fellowship, 1985.

Gilkey, Langdon. *Shantung Compound*. New York: Harper & Row, 1966.

Glines, Carroll V. *Doolittle's Tokyo Raiders*. New York: D. Van Nostrand Company, Inc., 1964.

—. *Four Came Home*. New York: D. Van Nostrand Company, Inc., 1966.

Gold, Hal. *Unit 731 Testimony*. Rutland, Vermont: Tuttle Publishing, 1997.

Goldstein, Norm. (Ed.). *China From the Long March to Tiananmen Square*. New York: Henry Holt and Company, 1990.

Greenough, Jan. *Courage in Dark Places*. London: Monarch Books, 2002a.

—. *Faith in Tough Places*. London: Monarch Books, 2002b.

Guinness, Geraldine. *The Story of the China Inland Mission, Volume I and II*. London: Morgan and Scott, 1894.

Hahn, Emily. *Chiang Kai-Shek*. New York: Doubleday & Company, 1955.

Harper, Damian. *National Geographic Traveler: China*. Barcelona, Spain: Cayfosa Quebecor, 2007.

Harris, Sheldon H. *Factories of Death*. New York: Routledge, 2002.

Hart, William J. *Unfamiliar Stories of Familiar Hymns*. Boston: W. A. Wilde Company, 1940.

Hefley, James and Marti. *The Secret File on John Birch*. Hannibal Books, 1995.

Henry, Carl F. H. (Ed.). *Basic Christian Doctrines*. New York: Holt, Rinehart and Winston, 1962.

Hu, Hua-ling. *American Goddess at the Rape of Nanking: The Courage of Minnie Vautrin*. Carbondale and Edwardsville: Southern Illinois University Press, 2000.

Hunter, Christine. *Gladys Aylward*. London: Coverdale House Publishers Ltd., 1971.

Jackson, Marjorie. *God's Prisoner of War*. Lancaster, Pennsylvania: Calvary Church Global Ministries, 2006.

Keller, W. Phillip. *Expendable!* Three Hills, Alberta: Prairie Press, 1966.

Kerr, Hugh T. *Children's Missionary Story-Sermons*. New York: Fleming H. Revell Company, 1915.

Kirk, Hector. *With God on the Prairies*. Three Hills, Alberta: Prairie Bible Institute, (Unknown date).

Kuhn, Isobel. *Ascent to the Tribes*. Littleton, Colorado: OMF International, 2010.

—. *Children of the Hills*. Littleton, CO: Overseas Missionary Fellowship, 2008.

—. *Green Leaf in Drought*. Singapore: OMF Books, 1958.

—. *Omnibus*. U.S.A.: OMF Publishing, 1997.

—. *Second-Mile People*. Singapore: Overseas Missionary Fellowship, 1982.

Lawson, Ted. *Thirty Seconds Over Tokyo*. New York: Pocket Star Books, 2002.

Locke, George H. (Ed.). "The World Book." Toronto: W.W. Quarrie & Company, 1923. pp. 5336–5337.

Magnusson, Sally. *The Flying Scotsman*. London: Quartet Books, 1981.

Marti-Ibanez, Felix. "On the Psychology of Buddhism." MD of Canada (1972): pp. 9–14.

Martin, Gordon. *Chefoo School 1881–1951*. Great Britain: Antony Rowe Ltd., 1990.

Martinson, Harold M. *Red Dragon Over China*. Minneapolis: Augsburg Publishing House, 1956.

Mathews, Arthur R. *Born for Battle*. Littleton, CO: OMF International, 2018.

McRoberts, Duncan. *Pleading China*. Grand Rapids, Michigan: Zondervan Publishing House, 1946.

—. *While China Bleeds*. Grand Rapids, Michigan: Zondervan Publishing House, 1943.

Melodies of Praise. Springfield, Missouri: Gospel Publishing House, 1957.

Michell, David. *A Boys War*. Overseas Missionary Fellowship, 1988.

—. *The Spirit of Eric Liddell*. Mississauga: OMF International, 1996.

Miller, Sheila. *Pigtails, Petticoats and the Old School Tie*. Belmont: OMF, 1981.

Mitter, Rana. *Forgotten Ally*. Boston: Houghton Mifflin Haricourt, 2013.

Morgan, Robert J. *Then Sings My Soul*. Nashville: W. Publishing, 2011.

Morse, Eugene. *Exodus to a Hidden Valley*. Glasgow: William Collins Sons & Co. Ltd., 1977.

Newell, Marvin J. *A Martyr's Grace*. Chicago: Moody Publishers, 2006.

OMF. *The China Awareness Seminar Handbook*. Littleton, CO: Overseas Missionary Fellowship, 1992.

Paulson, M. J. *Florence: A Missionary in China*. U.S.A.: M.J. Paulson Publishing, 2018.

Paulson, Philip. "Captured!" *Young Pilot* March and April 1965: pp. 24, 30–31; pp. 29–31.

Pollock, J. C. *Hudson Taylor and Maria.* U.S.A.: McGraw Hill, 1962.

Preston, Diana. *The Boxer Rebellion.* London: Robinson, 2002.

Scott, James M. *Target Tokyo.* New York: W. W. Norton & Company, 2015.

Scott, Munroe. McClure, *The China Years.* New York: Penguin Books, 1977.

Smith, Arthur. *China in Convulsion, Volumes One and Two.* London: Forgotten Books, 2017.

Society, Hillcrest Heritage. "Prairie Echoes." Calgary: Hillcrest Heritage Society, 1976. pp. 118–120.

Staff, The Peoples Gospel Hour. *Great Hymns and Their Stories.* Halifax, Nova Scotia: The Peoples Gospel Hour, (Unknown date).

Surhone, Lambert M., Tennoe, Miriam T. and Henssonow, Susan F. (Ed.). *Zhejiang-Jiangxi Campaign.* U.S.A.: Betascript Publishing, 2010.

Suyin, Han. *The Morning Deluge: Mao Tsetung & the Chinese Revolution, 1893–1954.* Boston: Little, Brown & Company, 1972.

Taylor, Dr. and Mrs. Howard. *Hudson Taylor and the China Inland Mission.* London: Lutterworth Press, 1952(b).

—. *Hudson Taylor in Early Years.* London: Lutterworth Press, 1952(a).

—. *Hudson Taylor's Spiritual Secret.* Chicago: Moody Press, 1932.

Taylor, Geraldine. *Behind the Ranges: The Story of J. O. Fraser.* Littleton, CO: OMF International, 2012.

—. *The Triumph of John and Betty Stam.* OMF International, 2012.

Taylor, Jay. *The Generalissimo.* Cambridge, Massachusetts: Harvard University Press, 2009.

Thiessen, Evangeline. *With Sails on His Bike.* Belleville, Ontario: Guardian Books, 2008.

Thompson, Phyllis. *China: The Reluctant Exodus.* U.S.A.: OMF International, 2000.

Thompson, R. E. and Ella. *Missionary Discipleship.* U.S.A.: Missionary Internship, 1982.

Thomson, H. C. *The Case for China*. London: C. T. Tinling & Co., Ltd., 1933.

Vautrin, Minnie. *Terror in Minnie Vautrin's Nanjing*. Chicago: University of Illinois Press, 2008.

Watson, Charles Hoyt. *De Shazer*. Winona Lake, Indiana: The Light and Life Press, 1950.

Watson, Jean. *Bosshardt A Biography*. OMF International, 1988.

Weatherby, W.J. *Chariots of Fire*. New York: Dell/Quicksilver, 1981.

Welch Jr., Robert H. W. *The Life of John Birch*. Appleton, Wisconsin: The John Birch Society, 1954.

White, Theodore H. *China: The Roots of Madness*. New York: W. W. Norton & Company Inc., 1968.

Wickert, Erwin. (Ed.). *The Good Man of Nanking: The Diaries of John Rabe*. New York: Vintage Books, 2000.

Wife, A Missionary's. *China and Its People*. London: James Nisbet & Co., 1862.

Wong, Jan. *Jan Wong's China*. Canada: Doubleday, 2000.

About the Author

Marguerite Joy Paulson is the youngest of seven children born to Florence and Clifford Paulson. She was given her second name, Joy, by her father who said the word Joy in the Bible had a special meaning for him because of her.

In 1972 Marguerite obtained a Bachelor of Arts degree in Sociology, and then travelled in Europe and Africa for a year, where she gained immeasurable life experience. Later, she obtained a Master of Science and a Doctoral degree from the University of Calgary. In 1987 she had the pleasure of accompanying her mother on a return trip to China.

In her professional life Marguerite has worked as a clinical and forensic psychologist, and is currently in private practice in a small rural community in northern Alberta.

She is thankful for being raised in a Christian home by God-fearing parents and for the example they provided of a life of integrity and love of others, in particular the Chinese people, and their faithfulness to God's calling. In the Bible it says, "Yea, a man may say, Thou hast faith, and I have works: shew me thy faith without thy works, and I will shew thee my faith by my works" (James 2:18). Her parents certainly expressed their faith by their actions and life.

Email: mjpaulson@abnorth.com

Acknowledgements

I would like to thank the following people whose assistance enabled me to fulfill my desire to write my father's story.

My brother, Duane, and his daughter, Deborah, for transcribing some of my father's sermon notes into literary form.

My brother-in-law, Rev. John Gishler, for his navigation through numerous maps for place names where my parents worked and the route they took in fleeing China.

My friend, L. P. Suzanne Atkinson, for her literary talent in the writing of my synopsis.

Robert Erion, a missionary to Thailand, in sharing his spiritual wisdom in dealing with demonic forces.

Andrew Wilmot for his meticulous copy-editing.

Donna Antkowiak for her creativity with the cover design and layout of the manuscript.

My two good friends and primary sources of support—Harriet Sawatzky for her editorial suggestions and typing of the manuscript and Barb Monita for her patience and assuming my responsibilities so that I could devote my time to writing.

All Scripture quotations are from the King James Version of the Bible, unless otherwise indicated.

Historical place names have been retained and are romanised in form.

Clifford's writings have been replicated as written, unless noted otherwise.

Newspaper articles have been reproduced from the original.

Maps are not drawn to scale and are included for reference purposes only.

www.ingramcontent.com/pod-product-compliance
Lightning Source LLC
Chambersburg PA
CBHW061148120626
46546CB00005B/1966